JavaScript Programming for Absolute Beginners

Ultimate Guide to JavaScript Coding, JavaScript

Programs and JavaScript Language

© Healthy Pragmatic Solutions Inc.
Copyright 2017 - All rights reserved.

The contents of this book may not be reproduced, duplicated or transmitted without direct written permission from the author.

Under no circumstances will any legal responsibility or blame be held against the publisher for any reparation, damages, or monetary loss due to the information herein, either directly or indirectly.

Legal Notice:

You cannot amend, distribute, sell, use, quote or paraphrase any part of the content within this book without the consent of the author.

Disclaimer Notice:

Please note the information contained within this document is for educational purposes only. No warranties of any kind are expressed or implied. Readers acknowledge that the author is not engaging in the rendering of legal, financial, medical or professional advice. Please consult a licensed professional before attempting any techniques outlined in this book.

By reading this document, the reader agrees that under no circumstances are is the author responsible for any losses, direct or indirect, which are incurred as a result of the use of information contained within this document, including, but not limited to, —errors, omissions, or inaccuracies.

Table of Contents

Introduction

Section 1: Setting Up Your Environment

Section 2: The Browser

  Your First JavaScript

  JavaScript Tag Placement

  External JavaScript Files

  The Browser Object Model

Section 3: Window Methods

  Window Methods and Events

  Window Events

  Document Object Model - DOM

Section 4: Programming Basics

  Variables

  Operator Precedence

  Conditional Logic

  IF ... ELSE

  IF ... ELSE IF

  Nested If Statements

  Comparison Operators

  Logical Operators

  The NOT Operator

- Switch Statements
- while loops

Section 5: Arrays and Functions

- Arrays
- Arrays and Loops
- Functions
- Functions That Call Other Functions
- Return Values
- Function Arguments
- Variable Scope

Section 6: String Manipulation

- Strings - Changing Case
- Strings - indexOf
- Strings - charAt
- Strings - substr
- Strings - Split and Join

Section 7: How JavaScript Works with HTML and CSS

Conclusion

JavaScript Mock Test Answers

Introduction

First, let me congratulate you for taking the time to read my guide to JavaScript. My intention is to guide you through the inner workings of JavaScript. I want you to learn exactly what JavaScript is, how it all works and how all the pieces fit together as well as going into some detail about some of the HTML elements that go together with JavaScript.

JavaScript is an incredibly light language and is easy to learn as well as being dynamic. Brendan Eich designed it in 1995 when he worked for Netscape, the owner of the very first web browser. JavaScript is a web-based programming language that is used for the creation of websites and web pages using other components like Java applets, images and plugins. JavaScript is an open source language and cross-platform and you will find that all the major websites use it as their core programming language.

To help you through, I have included lots of examples for you try yourself – this is the best way to learn something and I hope that it helps you too. There are also several exercises dotted throughout the book, just examples that you can have a go at. These are designed to compound what you have learned in a specific section and I haven't provided any answers for these. They are merely a way for you to practice and I would urge that you go over them over and again until you are confident. These are not just designed to test your knowledge of the subject but also to test whether you have learned the correct way to write the code. And, at the very end of the book, you will find a mock JavaScript test for you to try, complete with answers.

If you are ready to start learning JavaScript, let's go.

About The Series

"Javascript Programming For Absolute Beginners " is the another installment in this book series, meticulously developed by me and my passionate programming loving engineering team.

This series will provide you in depth insights and a full introduction to the world of javascript application.

Whenever we cover a new concept, topic or formula I ensure that a full in depth explanation is provided and push your understanding of the modern technology to a whole new level. Diagrams are provided to help maximize and visualize concepts, enhancing the learning process.

Please understand that this series will challenge your way of thinking. Especially, in later books we will dive into extremely technical topics that will inspire you.

I just need three things from you before we can begin. Please stay ***committed***, ***focused*** and ***passionate*** throughout the duration of all subject matter.

I have worked tirelessly structuring all this content together in the most practical, easy to read and step by step guide. I try to keep "high tech jargon" to a minimal and keep the flow of reading seamless and uninterrupted.

This is the first javascript programming publication officially released to the public - stay tuned for the newest releases by following my author page:

http://amzn.to/2xXVJqD

or simply find the author page directly under the book on Amazon.com

Feel free to comment and give feedback on potential new topics you'd like to learn about. I gather all input given by readers and take it into serious consideration when writing a new book.

Whenever you are ready, let's dive into javascript programming together! Turn the page. :)

Attribution - thanks to www.homeandlearn.co.uk for help with some of the code

*I'd like to give you a ***FREE e- book*** as my gift to you just see the link below. No strings attached. :) (If you can't find your confirmation e-mail, try looking in your junk mail)

http://bit.ly/2yFU3B0

Simply as a 'thank you' for downloading this book, this link will give you free access to an exclusive service that will send you notifications when Amazon's Best sellers are released, are on discount price or go on FREE promotion. If you are someone who is interested in saving a TON of money, simply click the FREE e- book link above.

As an added bonus...I would like to invite you to join my exclusive GROUP. You will be a part of a community of programming & technology experts/enthusiast.

The added benefit to this is you will have access to my most recent and newest bestselling books on the market for FREEE!

I have a new book coming out soon and you don't want to miss out!

Join my exclusive group by clicking the link below...

http://bit.ly/2gzY2c1

Join now!

Section 1: Setting Up Your Environment

Before you can even begin to write any JavaScript, you are going to need a couple of things – a text editor and a decent web browser that contains tools for web development. For this, we are going to use the Chrome browser and look at a text editor called Brackets.

Chrome

One of the most important things about learning JavaScript is learning the console and that includes how to set it up. Chrome has its own built-in console and this is perfect for inputting your scripts and code – even better, it's free. This is how you get it:

   1. Open the web browser you are using and type in www.google.com/Chrome

2. Download the Chrome browser. From here, it is your choice as to whether you keep Chrome as your primary browser or you just use it for doing your JavaScript. Follow all the on-screen instructions to download and install Chrome browser
3. Open the Chrome browser and look for an Options circle in the top right corner – click it and you will see some more options
4. Select More Tools and then Developer Tools
5. Now select Console and the console pad will load. You should see the symbol > on it – this is your command prompt and it is where all your code will be input.

Now you can begin to use the console in Chrome so take the time out to explore it; learn what it is all about and how to use it.

Shortcut

There is a shortcut to open your console:

- Download and install Chrome
- In the address bar, type about: blank and a blank page will load

Getting Started

Now that you have set up your console, you can type console.log() at your command prompt – this will log you in. Now is the time to begin exploring and learn what JavaScript is all about – as I mentioned earlier, you will find lots of practical examples to help you out through the book so use them and learn. A couple of helpful hints – you can click the button that says Preserve Log to preserve anything that you input and if you want to save your work, right-click anywhere in the console and choose Save As.

Now let's look at text editors. You can choose any that you want but I would recommend Brackets

Brackets

Brackets is open source and is specifically designed for web development. It is built using JavaScript making it the very best editor, providing plenty of useful tools and help for you to learn how to code much easier and much more effectively.

1. Open your web browser and type in http://brackets.io/
2. Download the version that corresponds to your operating system – Linux, Windows or Mac

When you open Brackets for the first time, you will be presented with a project named "Getting Started." Onscreen instructions will show you how to use the features in Brackets

- Opening a folder is simple – click File>Open Folder. You will see this in the file tree that is to the left of your screen. This is your projects folder and it has some settings related to it. To move between projects, simply click on the root folder name in the tree or you can drag the relevant folder form your operating system into Brackets and it will open.

- Instead of showing your opened files in tabs, Brackets shows them in a list titles "Working Files" and you will find this above the tree. Clicking on a file in that tree will allow you to view the file but it won't get put into the Working Files List. This way, you can look through the files without having to open each one. Any changes that are made to a file will be put automatically into the Working Files list and to add a file to the list without having to edit it first, you simply double-click the name.

To begin with, a single editor will be on show in Brackets view but you can split it so you see two editors. These can be horizontal or vertical and to choose, click View and then on Horizontal Split or Vertical Split. The main view will now show as two and you can view two files at the same time. You will also get another Working Files list so you can see what is open in each pane. You can also drag files between the two panes.

Brackets is very clever in that, whatever view layout you had for each project, it will remember it. Opening a project will show you which layout was there when you saved and closed the project. To close split view and go back to a single pane, just click on View and then on No Split. You won't shut down any open files by doing this; the separate lists of Working Files will now be merged into one and all changes will be stored until you chose to discard or to save them.

Have a play, learn your way around Brackets and then open a new console, ready to start coding.

Section 2: The Browser

Your First JavaScript

Open your text editor and input the following:

```
<!DOCTYPE HTML>

<HTML>

<HEAD>

<TITLE>-A First Script</TITLE>

</HEAD>

<BODY>

</BODY>

</HTML>
```

Here we have the beginnings of your webpage – the HEAD and BODY tags and the TITLE area. Save this as first_script.html. A word of note – if you use Notepad as your Editor, change Save As to All File Types otherwise you will have a text file and not an HTML page.

Next, we are going to add some tags so, in-between the BODY tags, type in:

<SCRIPT LANGUAGE = "Javascript">

alert("Hello World")

</SCRIPT>

You always add a program script between the opening and closing <SCRIPT> tags. One of the SCRIPT tag attributes is called LANGUAGE and this is what tells your browser the name of the script language that is in use – in our case, this is JavaScript. This is added after the = sign – note that the word JavaScript has been enclosed in double quotation marks. This isn't absolutely necessary, you could even skip the LANGUAGE attribute altogether and have this:

<SCRIPT>

alert("Hello World")

</SCRIPT>

```
<!DOCTYPE HTML>
<HTML>
        <HEAD>
                  <TITLE>A First Script</TITLE>
        </HEAD>

        <BODY>
                  <SCRIPT LANGUAGE = "Javascript">
                        alert("Hello World")
                  </SCRIPT>

        </BODY>
</HTML>
```

Do note that if you omit the forward slash at the start of the closing SCRIPT tag your code is not going to work. As you can with all HTML tags, your SCRIPT tags may be written in lowercase, if it is easier for you, like this:

<script>

alert("Hello World")

</script>

Another note – while SCRIPT tags do not follow case sensitivity, JavaScript does. The code we have written is one line and all it is doing is displaying a popup dialog box that shows the words, "Hello, World". Have a go at it. Make sure you save your works and then use Windows Explorer or Windows or Finder on the Mac to go to where the HTML file was saved. Double-click the file to run it in the browser

Change the alert line to read:

Alert("Hello World")

Note that alert is now started with a capitalized 'A'. Save and load the page in the browser again and you will notice that the box now no longer shows up. Change back to a lowercase 'a', save, reload and the box will reappear.

These Alert boxes display information to website users. Between the round brackets, you input what text you want the user to see and make sure it is in between a set of quote marks – use single or double, not a combination.

Confirm and Prompt

You can also have Confirm and Prompt boxes – the Confirm box will give you an OK and a Cancel button and these are generally used with IF statements to determine which button is clicked. More about IF statement later but, to get a confirm box, simply type in:

confirm("OK or Cancel?")

Again, the text must be inserted between quotation marks.

Prompt boxes are used when you need the user to input something. This is the code for the prompt box:

prompt("Favorite animal?", "Cat")

Note that there are two bits in between the round brackets – first the heading and then the default text.

Users will input text into a box on the dialog box and when they press the OK button, you get the input text and can do something with it – you will see more about this when we look at IF statements later. For both these two boxes, Confirm and Prompt, you must use lowercase letters.

Next, we are going to look at the placement of JavaScript tags.

JavaScript Tag Placement

There are three places where you can insert a SCRIPT tag:

- Between two BODY tags
- Between two HEAD tags
- In the HEAD section as a link to an external file

Some say that the SCRIPT tags should go at the end of the BODY section, like this:

<!DOCTYPE HTML>

<HTML>

<HEAD>

<TITLE>A First Script</TITLE>

</HEAD>

<BODY>

HTML GOES HERE. JAVSCRIPT GOES AFTER HTML

<SCRIPT LANGUAGE = "Javascript"›

confirm("OK or Cancel?")

</SCRIPT>

</BODY>

</HTML>

We do it this way because the web page will load before any script gets read – if the tag is in the HEAD section, the script gets parsed before the CSS or HTML elements get loaded.

Most of the time, script tags are better placed in the HEAD section, like this:

<!DOCTYPE HTML>

<HTML>

<HEAD>

</HEAD>

<BODY>

</BODY>

</HTML>

<TITLE>A First Script</TITLE>

```
<SCRIPT LANGUAGE = "Javascript">

confirm("OK or Cancel?")

</SCRIPT>
```

```
<!DOCTYPE HTML>
<HTML>
        <HEAD>
                <TITLE>A First Script</TITLE>

                <SCRIPT LANGUAGE = "Javascript">
                        confirm("OK or Cancel?")
                </SCRIPT>
        </HEAD>

        <BODY>

        </BODY>
</HTML>
```

Exercise

Using the code from the last lesson, take the code from the BODY and put it into the HEAD section so that it looks something like the code above. Then, change the Confirm box so it is an alert message.

External JavaScript Files

You can also put your code into an external file and your SCRIPT tags will have an SRC attribute – this will show the location of the file. This is the code:

<HEAD>

<TITLE>A First Script</TITLE>

<SCRIPT LANGUAGE = "Javascript"

</SCRIPT>

</HEAD>

In this code, the following attributes have been added into the opening SCRIPT tag:

SRC="scripts/external_javascript.js"

SRC is short for Source. You have an = sign followed by the path that leads to the file. In this case, we have created a file named external_javasctipt.js and put it in a folder named scripts. Note that, when you save code to an external file location, you must have the .js extension at the end of the file name.

The actual file is:

'alert("External Javascript File-)

What we have here is nothing more than an alert box line. There are no SCRIPT tags in the file because they are already in the HTML. When the HTML is parsed by the browser, it can see the SRC attribute and it will then add in all the JavaScript.

If your code starts to get a little too long and somewhat unwieldy, you can control it better by putting it into an external file. Not only that, you can easily make changes by editing just a single file instead of having to change the HEAD section in multiple HTML files.

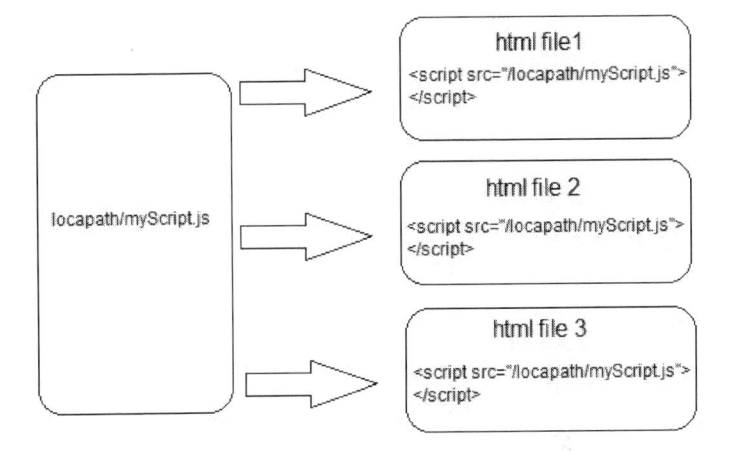

```
                                    html file 1
                              <script src="/locapath/myScript.js">
                              </script>

                                    html file 2
locapath/myScript.js          <script src="/locapath/myScript.js">
                              </script>

                                    html file 3
                              <script src="/locapath/myScript.js">
                              </script>
```

Exercise

Move the alert message over to an external file and ensure that the referencing bit, that comes after SRC, is correct – if not, the code will not run correctly.

The Browser Object Model

Every browser is split up into separate parts or objects that may be accessed through JavaScript. As a whole, these objects are called the BOM or Browser Object Model, and at the top is the Window object. This object is representative of the whole browser – the menus, the toolbars, the entire page and everything on it.

Beneath this Window object you will find lots more different objects which allow you to carry out other tasks, like redirecting users, get the browser window size, access every HTML element on the page, and a good deal more besides. The following are some of the more popular Windows objects:

- **window.document** – lets you access all the HTML elements
- **window.history** – allows you to access browsing history information. This is limited in use because you are not able to see which pages your users have visited, only the number of pages in the history. Other methods that you could access, if you wanted to, are history.forward, history.back and history.go.
- **window.innerHeight/window.innerWidth** – gives you information about the available space on your page
- **window.screen** – provides information about the browser screen

You could be forgiven for confusing the screen with width and height but they are two different things. Let's try an example to show you this; create an HTML page using SCRIPT tags placed in the HEAD section and then add in the following code:

```
<!DOCTYPE HTML> <HTML>

<HEAD>

<TITLE>-The window object</TITLE>

<SCRIPT LANGUAGE = -javascript->
alert(window.innerHeight) </SCRIPT>

</HEAD> <BODY> </BODY>

</HTML>
```

This is just an alert box that has window.innerHeight inserted in between brackets. Before, we had text in the brackets inside a set of double quotes. Save the page and then load it up in your browser.

Next, cut the browser size. If you are using Windows, click the icon for Restore Down; Mac users can use the mouse pointer to do this

Press F5 to refresh the page and you should now see the innerHeight value change to the new value.

Now you can change the code for the alert box to this:

alert(window.screen.height)

Now we are using the screen object's height value so save and refresh.

- **window.navigator** – this one is used for getting browser information.

The Navigator object will also show you a number of other objects that you can use, such as:

- **window.navigator.cookieEnabled** – Insert this in between round brackets for an alert box and it will inform you if cookies are enabled in your browser. We would normally use this inside an IF statement – if the answer were YES, the cookie is set on the browser. If NO, you ask the user to enable cookies.

Other navigator objects you can use include:
appName
appVersion
language
platform
userAgent

Have a go at using these in an alert box and look at what each one does.

- **window.location** – this object lets you do some pretty advanced stuff but, mainly, we use it to redirect users to another page. We use it with code like this:

window.location = "http://www.homeandlearn.co.uk/";

After the = sign, you input the name of the website that you want your visitors redirected to and ensure that the name is inserted between quotes and use a semicolon at the end of the statement. Although this isn't really needed here, you should always use a semicolon to separate code lines.

That's it for this section, next we are going to look at Window methods.

```
                        ┌─────────────────────────────────┐
                        │            Window               │
                        ├──────┬────────┬──────┬──────────┤
                        │frame │ parent │ self │   top    │
                        └──────┴────────┴──────┴──────────┘
```

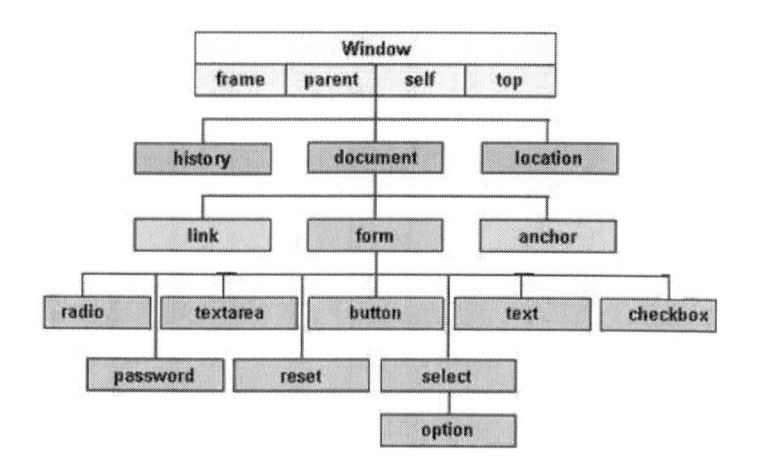

- history
- document
- location
- link
- form
- anchor
- radio
- textarea
- button
- text
- checkbox
- password
- reset
- select
- option

Section 3: Window Methods

Window Methods and Events

Going back to the Window Object, it also has Methods and these are code chunks that do something specific Think back to the three boxes we used in the last chapter – Alert, Confirm and Prompt. All of these are methods and, if we're to be very specific, what we would have written would be:

window.alert("Alert Message")

And also, this:

window.confirm("OK or Cancel")

However, the Window object is also known as a global object and that means there is no need for the window. (dot) notation – all you need to do is type in the bit after that. However, at least when you are just beginning, you should include the window section as it makes your code much clearer.

Some of the other common window methods are:

window.clearInterval
window.clearTimeout
window.setInterval
window.setTimeout

window.close
window.open
window.print

The first four are used for setting and manipulating timers and these are useful for animations. Close and Open do just what they say – close and open windows while the Print method will bring up the print dialog box. We're going to look a bit closer at the window.open method.

window.open

Sometimes it can be very useful to be able to open a new window from the one you are currently in. These new windows usually open when a hyperlink on the web page is clicked and you may also have one open when the website is loaded up – these are known as popups and are quite annoying for site visitors.

The following code shows you how a new window is opened when a particular hyperlink is clicked. Do not worry if you don't get this code yet, it is a little complicated for you right now. The reason I want to show you this know is because it uses something that you will be learning about later on – a function, which gets called when the link is clicked.

```
<!DOCTYPE HTML>

<HTML>

<HEAD>

</HTML>

</HEAD>

<BODY>
```

```
</BODY>
<TITLE>Window open method</TTTLE>
<SCRIPT LANGUAGE = "Javascript">
function eAdd() f
var msgwindow = window.open("popup.html",
"Popup",
"toolbar=no,width=500,height=300");
</SCRIPT>
<a href="#" onclick="eAdd()">Link Text Here</A>
```

The part of the above code that opens the window is:

```
window.open("popup.html",
"PopUp",
"toolbar=no,width=500,height=300");
```

Note that, between the brackets for open, there are three things:

- The page you want in the new window
- A name for the window
- Window configuration options

There are three options for configuration – one that sets the toolbar to no, the width and then the height of the window. All of these options must go inside quotation marks and there must be no spaces between the option and the value. Each is separated by a comma.

Window Events

We used a hyperlink to open the new window in the previous section and that hyperlink was placed between the BODY tags and this was the text we used:

<a href="#" onClick="eAdd()">Link Text Here</A>

onClick is known as an event and there are a lot of objects that go in between the BODY tags that may use this event. Examples include images, buttons n forms, drop-down lists, checkboxes, etc. However, the idea is to call a piece of code into action whenever that event happens.

There are quite a few different events that you can use and most are self-explanatory:

onChange
onClose
onKeydown
onKeypress
onKeyup
onLoad
onMousedown
onMousemove

onMouseout
onMouseover
onMouseup
onScroll
onSelect
onSubmit
onUnload

You will meet many of these throughout the course of this book and they will be explained as we come to them. Next, we will look at Document, one of the most important window objects.

Document Object Model - DOM

Document is another of the Window objects that may be manipulated. It is a very powerful object that refers to pretty much every element that may be on your web page. What this means is that JavaScript may be used to access, amend and add new HTML elements. However, this is advanced so we are going to look the most useful one - document.write.

document.write

This method may be used for inserting text onto your web page so try this example:

- Create a new HTML web page
- Save it and call it write_method.html
- Add this H1 heading into the HTML - <Hi>The document.write method</H1>
- Place two tags into the Body section
- Between the SCRIPT tags, input this – document.write(window.screen.height);

Your page and code should look something like this:

<! TYPE HTML>

```
<HTML>
<HEAD>
</HEAD>
<BODY>
</BODY>
</HTML>
<TITLE>The write
<H1>The document.
<SCRIPT LANGUAGE
document.
</SCRIPT>
method</TITLE>
write method</H1>
= "Javascript">
write(window.screen.height);
```

Now save it and open it in a web browser.

Note that, rather than an alert box, we have now written the height of the screen straight to the page.

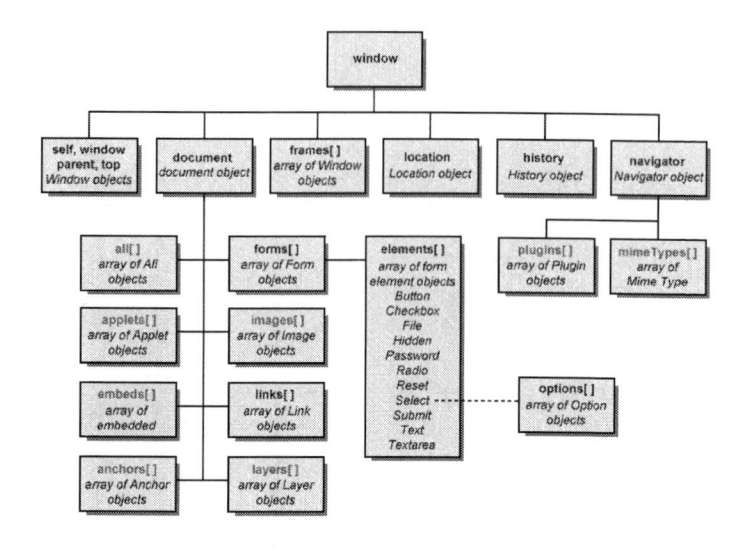

Cut the JavaScript section form BODY and paste it to HEAD, save and then refresh the page in the browser.

Now your screen height is at the top and this is because the HEAD section is always the first to be executed. However, the browser won't wait for the page to load, it will execute the HEAD code first and, in our case, the code contained the method document.write. Because this method will write to the page, this will happen before any of the HTML will be displayed.

Now put the code back into the BODY and amend it to this:

document.write("Screen Height=" + window.screen.height);

What we have here is something called concatenation. All this means is that we have joined two strings of text together. Note that a little direct code has been placed between quotation marks and, following the + we have input the code for the screen height. The + symbol, when we use it in this context, literally means, "add together." You can use this as often as you want, for example:

document.write("SH=" + window.screen.height + " SW=" + window.screen.width);

SH means screen height and SW is screen width but note the spaces and commas where the plus signs are. If you don't get these right, your code isn't going to work.

HTML tags may be used with concatenation. Let's say you want to put something over a couple of lines; you would use the BR tag, just like this:

document.write("SH=" + window.screen.height + "<BR>" + "SW=" + window.screen.width);

Note that BR is enclosed in quote marks and these must be used for any of the HTML that is inserted with the write method.

You may use the document.write method as many times as you need to. Look at the following example; the SCRIPT tags have been moved to the HEAD section and document.write has been used two times – once in the H1 line and once for adding the text below it.

<!DOCTYPE HTML> <HTML>

<HEAD>

<TITLE>The Write Method</TITLE>

<SCRIPT LANGUAGE = "Javascript">

document.write("<H1>The write method</H1>"); document.write("screen Height=" + window. screen. height); </SCRIPT>

</HEAD> <BODY> </BODY>

</HTML>

In the next section, we will look at Variables and many of the other concepts that make up the code.

Section 4: Programming Basics
This is a very long section so make sure you understand each part before you move on to the next

Variables
A variable is exactly the same, no matter which programming language you use. They are, in essence, storage places where things are placed for later retrieval. Think of them as small boxes; you write an important piece of information on paper and store it in the box. Give the box a name that relates to the contents and you can easily retrieve the information when you need it.

When you set a variable up in JavaScript, you begin it with var, followed by a space and then a name for the variable. You can name it pretty much anything you want but you must follow the rules for naming:

- There can be no spaces in the variable name

- The variable name may not begin with a number
- The name can only have letters, numbers, an underscore (_) and a dollar sign ($)

Valid names include:

number2

my_phone_number

$familyName

While invalid names are:

2number

my phone number

"familyName"

As a word of advice, do not start any variable name with a number, have any spaces in them or use quote marks.

To store information in a variable we use the = symbol. You can store all sorts in there, numbers, Boolean values, and strings of text. These are all known as primitive data types but you can also store an object in a variable, such as the Document, Navigator and Window objects we met earlier.

```html
<!DOCTYPE HTML>
<HTML>
        <HEAD>
                <TITLE>Variables</TITLE>

                <SCRIPT LANGUAGE = "Javascript">

                        var number1 = 42;
                        var true_or_false = true;
                        var firstName = 'Kenny';

                </SCRIPT>
        </HEAD>

        <BODY>

        </BODY>
</HTML>
```

Let's get our hands dirty a little.

First, create a brand-new web page and add JavaScript tags to the HEAD section and, between the Javascript tags set up these three variables with their values:

var number1 = 42;
var true_or_false = true;
var firstName = 'Kenny';

So, we now have three variables, all of which begin with the var keyword. The first stores a numerical value of 25, the second has a Boolean value of true and the third, a text value of 'Johnny." Note that the first two do not require quotations but any text strings must be enclosed in single or double quotes.

Next, add in these lines:

document.write(number1 + "<BR>");
document.write(true_or_false + "<BR>");
document.write(firstName + "<BR>");

```
<!DOCTYPE HTML>
<HTML>
    <HEAD>
            <TITLE>Variables</TITLE>

            <SCRIPT LANGUAGE = "Javascript">

                var number1 = 42;
                var true_or_false = true;
                var firstName = 'Kenny';

                document.write(number1 + "<BR>");
                document.write(true_or_false + "<BR>");
                document.write(firstName + "<BR>");

            </SCRIPT>
    </HEAD>

    <BODY>

    </BODY>
</HTML>
```

We have used document.write so that we can access the values of the variables.
 just ensures that each variable gets printed on its own line. Your code should look something like this:

<!DOCTYPE HTML> <HTML> <HEAD>

</HTML>

</HEAD>

<BODY>

</BODY>

```
<TITLE>variables</TITLE> <SCRIPT
LANGUAGE = "Javascript"> var numberl = 25;
var true_or_false = true; var firstName =
'Johnny'; document.write(numberl + "<Blz>");
document.write(true_or_false + "<Bft);
document.write(firstName + "<Bft>");

</SCRIPT>
```

Do be sure that each of the lines ends with the semicolon and that there is a space between var and the name of the variable. There isn't any need to insert spaces either side of the = symbol but it does help make your code easier to read.

Save the work and then load up the webpage. You should see this:

25
true
Johnny

So, what have we done here? We stored three different values inside three different values and, to retrieve those values we used only the variable name. You can also use concatenation to join variable names together, like this:

document.write("The variable contains a value of: " + number1 + "<BR>");

Here, we concatenated the text "The variable contains a value of" with the variable called number1. We used the + sign to do the concatenation. Have a go yourself. Use the document.write code so that it looks like:

```
document.write( "The variable contains a value of: " + number1 + "<BR>");
document.write( "Is it true or false? " + true_or_false + "<BR>");
document.write( "What is your first name? " + firstName + "<BR>");
```

Do be sure that the + symbols and the quotation marks are in the correct places or else nothing will work. Single quotes work just as well as double quotes, just make sure you use the same at the finish as you do the start.

Save and then load the web page – you should see this:

The variable contains a value of: 25.

Is it true or false? true

What is your first name?

Johnny

Variable Assignment

When we set the variable, we did it like this:

```
var number1 = 25;
```

But there is no need to store values in the variable on the same line; you can do it over two lines:

```
var number1;
number1 = 25;
```

Line 1 creates the variable named number1 but there isn't any value stored inside it. Line 2 is where the value is stored – note that we didn't use var this time. This is only required when you set the variable up, not the value.

You may also assign different values to variables, like this:

```
var number1;
number1 = 25;
number1 = 150;
```

Because JavaScript is a sequential language, the code is executed one line at a time, top to bottom. What we did here was to assign the variable with a value of 25 and then stored another new number in the variable. When a new value is stored, the old one is removed so the variable called number1 will now have a value of 150, not 25.

You can also use a text string to overwrite the value, like this:

```
var number1;
number1 = 25;
number1 = "one hundred and fifty";
```

This time, we stored the text, "one hundred and fifty" in the variable even though the previous value was a number. No other programming language will do this and you would get an error – JavaScript doesn't much care though so you can do it.

In the next section, we are going to look at mathematical operators.

Mathematical Operators

```
<!DOCTYPE HTML>
<HTML>
        <HEAD>
                <TITLE>Mathematical Operators</TITLE>
                <SCRIPT LANGUAGE = "Javascript">
                        var number1 = 42;
                        var number2 = 100;
                        var total;

                        total = number1 + number2;

                        document.write( total );
                </SCRIPT>
        </HEAD>
        <BODY>

        </BODY>
</HTML>
```

We use the mathematical operators with the variables so that you can add, subtract, multiply and divide. These are the symbols:

- Plus (+) is for addition
- Minus (-) is for subtraction
- Asterisk (*) is for multiplication
- Forward (/) is for division
- Percentage (%) is for modulus calculations

Let's get a little practice with thee. Create yourself a new web page or use the one you created in the last section. Now add in two

Javascript tags to the HEAD section and in between them input this code:

```
var number1 = 25;
var number2 = 150;
var total;

total = number1 + number2;
document.write( total );
```

Your code should look something like this:

<!DOCTYPE HTML> <HTML> <HEAD> <TITLE>Mathematical Operators</TITLE> <SCRIPT LANGUAGE = "Javascript> var numberl = 25; var number 2 - 150; var total; total = numberl + number2; document.write(total);

</SCRIPT>

</HEAD>

<BODY>

<(BODY>

<HTML>

Save and load the webpage. You should see the number 175 on the page. If not, double check your code.

We stored the numbers 25 and 150 in two separate variables called number1 and number2. Then we set the third one up that we called total. The 4th code line says this:

total = number1 + number2;

On the right of the = sign are the two variables, separated by the + sign. This time, that + is not being used for concatenation, it is being used for addition. JavaScript knows when the variables both contain numbers so it knows to add and not join them. An example – place quote marks around 150:

var number2 = "150";

Save and then open the web page and you will see this:

25150

Because you place the number in quotes, you have turned it into text so JavaScript concatenates the two, rather than adding them.

Try these exercises:

Exercise

Take away the quote marks from 150 and then change + into -. Save the changes and refresh your browser. What do you get?

Exercise

Now change – into *, save and refresh. What is your total now?

Exercise

Change + to /, save and refresh. What do you get now?

You may use normal numbers with these operators. Look at the next code – we add two numbers and store the resulting number in a variable:

var result;
result = 12 + 36;
document.write(result);

JavaScript adds the numbers on the right side of the = symbol and stores the results in a variable on the left.

Storing Objects in Variables

Previously, we used document.write and an alert message with the different objects, something like this:

alert (window.innerWidth);

These values may also be stored in variables. If for example, you wanted the value of innerWidth stored in a variable, you would do this:

var width = window.innerWidth;

When the value is stored, you can do other things later.

alert(width);

In the next section, we look at operator precedence.

Operator Precedence

Operator precedence

Level	Operators	Notes
1	() [] .	call, member (including typeof and void)
2	! ~ - ++ --	negation, increment
3	* / %	multiply/divide
4	+ -	addition/subtraction
5	<< >> >>>	bitwise shift
6	< <= > >=	relational
7	== !=	equality
8	&	bitwise AND
9	^	bitwise XOR
10	|	bitwise OR
11	&&	logical AND
12	||	logical OR
13	?:	conditional
14	= += -= *= /= %= <<= >>= >>>= &= ^= |=	assignment
15	,	comma

You can use more than two numbers if you want and you can mix up numbers and variables. Edit the total line in your code so it reads like this:

total = number1 + number2 / 2;

This time, we are using a division symbol and then a 2 at the end of the line. What do you think the result will be? You could be forgiven for thinking that JavaScript will add the two numbers and then divide by 2 but it won't. To tell JavaScript what you want it to do, you need to use brackets. If you want the addition done before the division, write your code like this:

total = (number1 + number2) / 2;

JavaScript will now carry out the sum between the brackets and will then divide the answer by 2. If on the other hand, you wanted the second number divided by 2 and then added to the first number, you just change the brackets, like this:

total = number1 + (number2 / 2) ;

We do this because of operator precedence. This means that we determine which mathematical symbols are actioned first. Look at this code:

var result = 4 + 9 * 7

The * or multiplication operator has got a higher priority than addition (+) so because the 9 and the 7 are together, JavaScript wants to multiply these two numbers together to give 63 and then add the 4 to give 67. To override the precedence, you use the brackets so, if you wanted 4 and 9 added and then multiplied by 7, you would do this:

var result = (4 + 9) * 7

Now the result is 91 — (4 + 9 equals 13, multiplied by 7 gives 91.

Multiplication and division are treated equally and both take priority over subtraction and addition, both of which are also equal in priority to one another. Let's make that a little clearer:

var result = 32 - 16 / 8

Division is higher in precedence than subtraction so JavaScript first divides 16 by 8 to give 2 and then it subtracts that form 32 to give a result of 30. Now, if you add in some brackets:

var result = (32 - 16) / 8

This time, Javascript sees the brackets and does that calculation first so 32 — 16 gives a result of 16, which is then divided by the 8 to get 2.

Take this sum:

var result = 32 - 16 + 8;

Remember, subtraction and addition have got the same priority so this sum gets calculated left to right and the answer is 24. However, add in some brackets and we get a different answer:

```
var result = 32 - (16 + 8);
```

In this sum, the calculation between the brackets is done first, providing a result of 24 which is then subtracted from 32, providing a result of 8.

Be very careful when you use operators because you might not get the result you want!

We haven't yet discussed the modulus operator. If you don't know what a modulus is, it is the remainder when one number is divided by another. For example, normally, if you divided, let's say, 41 by 10, you would get an answer of 4.1 – 10 will divide into 41 4 times with a remainder of 1. Modulus holds onto that 1 and discards the rest but why? Simply because modulus will tell you if a number is even or odd. Divide a number by 2 – if there is a remainder, that number is an odd one. Have a look at this code:

```
var result = 41 % 2;

if (result == 1) {
document.write("Odd number");
}
else {
document.write("Even number");
}
```

We haven't covered the IF statement yet but, even so, you should still be able to figure out what is going on here. We tested a number with the modulus operator and then say IF the modulus has a value of 1, "Odd number should be written, ELSE, "Even number" gets written.

Next, we are going to look at conditional logic.

Conditional Logic

Earlier, you learned that JavaScript is sequential which means it executes code in sequence, as it is written. Sometimes, you won't want every line executed and you want to be able to control how your programming works.

One way to do this is using conditional logic which is where the IF statement comes in. Conditional logic is about what would happen IF a specified condition is or isn't met.

IF Statement

IF statements are ideal for when you want to control how your code flows. IF statements only evaluate either True or False and they look like this:

if (condition_to_test) {

}

Basically, an if statement consists of the word 'if' in lowercase letters, followed by the condition to test inside a pair of round brackets. That condition gets evaluated to see if it is true. If it is then the code that is in between the curly brackets will be executed. If the condition evaluates false, then that code is ignored. Have a look at the following example:

var first_name = "Johnny";

if (first_name == "Johnny") {

document.write("First Name is Johnny " + first_name);

}

The first line of this code is storing a text string of "Johnny" in a variable named first_name. Then we have the IF statement and the condition to be tested is in between the round brackets:

first_name == "Johnny"

We check to see if the variable named first name has got the word "Johnny" in it. Note that there are two == symbols between the variable and the text. This double == symbol means "has a value of". It is not assigning the value of "Johnny" to the variable as it would if we had just a single = symbol so, the entire line reads "IF the variable called first name has a value of Johnny." JavaScript tests that statement to see if it is true – if it is, the code between those curly brackets will be executed.

Try the code out for yourself. Create your new web page and then type in the above code between the JavaScript tags – it should look like this:

<!DOCTYPE HTML>

<HTML>

<HEAD>

<TITLE>Basic If Statement</TITLE>

<SCRIPT LANGUAGE = "Javascript"> var first_name = "Johnny";

if (first_name —"Johnny") {

document.write("First Name is Johnny " + first_name);

</SCRIPT>

</HEAD>

<BODY>

</BODY>

</HTML>

Do make sure that you have the right format for the IF statements. The first line only requires a single = symbol because you are assigning the variable with the value of "Johnny." Between the round brackets in the IF statement, you require two == symbols and you also require a pair of curly brackets – this is where your code is going.

Save and open the page in a browser; you should see this:

First Name is Johnny Johnny

Why have we got Johnny down twice? The first one is because "Johnny" was typed between double quotes and the second is because JavaScript always writes the value of the variable called first_name.

Delete one of those == symbols from the round brackets and change Johnny to Billy

if (first_name = "Billy") {

Save, and open in the browser. This time, you should see this:

First Name is Johnny Lenny

Although the value of "Johnny" was assigned to the variable in line 1, it was changed by

JavaScript to "Billy" and it did this because we removed one = symbol from the double == symbols in the IF statement. This automatically assigns the variable with a new value.

Be careful when you do your conditions in between round brackets in an IF statement – two == symbols will check the value while a single = symbol assigns the value.

Next, we are going to look at the IF...ELSE statement.

IF ... ELSE

You can also put an ELSE bit into your IF statement, useful for when you want to control what will happen if the IF statement is False. Change the code you wrote to this:

var first_name = "Sammy";

if (first_name == "Johnny") {

document.write("First Name is " + first_name);

}

else {

document.write("First Name is " + first_name);

}

The first line changed "Johnny" to "Sammy" and between those curly brackets, we now see:

document.write("First Name is " + first_name);

Take a look at the ELSE bit:

else {

document.write("First Name is " + first_name);

}

If you add ELSE to your IF statement, it must have its own curly brackets – omit one and your code is not going to work. Save the changes, run the code and you should see this:

First Name is Sammy

The first bit of the IF statement is checking the condition that is in the round brackets. If it evaluates true, the code in the curly brackets of the IF statement is executed. If it is false, JavaScript goes straight to the ELSE bit and executes the code in the curly brackets for the ELSE statement.

IF ... ELSE IF
There is one more condition that you can add – the ELSE IF statement, which looks like this:

if (first_condition_to_test) {

}

else if (second_condition_to_test) {

}

Note that ELSE IF is in two words – type it as one word (ELSSEIF) and your code isn't going to work. Basically, it is an IF statement that has the word ELSE added to the front.

You can have as many ELSE parts to your statement as you need:

if (first_condition_to_test) {

}

else if (second_condition_to_test) {

}

else if (third_condition_to_test) {

}

Each condition evaluates true or false – if a true value is found, the code in the curly brackets for that statement will be executed and the IF statement will be exited, skipping any remaining conditions.

You may also have an ELSE at the end of your statement just in case there is something else you want to check for:

if (first_condition_to_test) {

}

```
else if ( second_condition_to_test ) {

}

else if ( third_condition_to_test ) {

}

else {

}
```

Try this example:

```
<SCRIPT LANGUAGE = "Javascript"> var first_name = "Ginny";

if (first_name      "Johnny") -[

document.write('First IF " + first_name);

}

else if (first_name = "Sammy")
document.write("Second IF " + first_name);

else if (first_name = "Lenny") -[
document.write("Third IF " + first_name);

else 1

document.write("ELSE PART " + first_name);

</SCRIPT>
```

Now, the first line has assigned the first_name variable with a value of "Ginny" so you should be able to work out what is executed.

Try this exercise:

Exercise

Change "Ginny" into "Johnny" and then change it to "Sammy" and finally "Lenny" just to see what will be printed each time. Now change the uppercase S on Sammy to a lowercase s, giving you sammy – what will be printed?

Nested If Statements

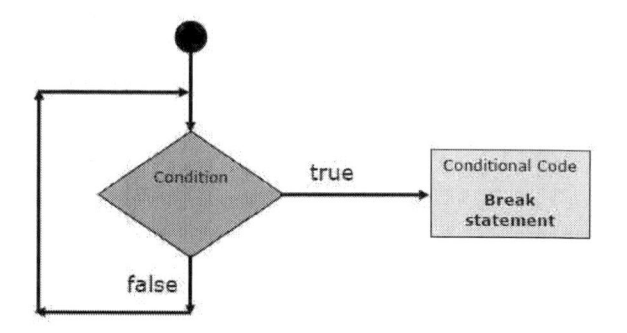

You may nest IF statements if you want to. Let's say that you want to test out a variable to find out the value in it but you will also want to do other things on it as well. You would do something like this:

if (x > 1) {

if (x == 2) {

}

else if (x == 3) {

}

}

In this code, we test the variable called x to see if it is greater than 1 but we also want to narrow this down a little. If it is greater than 1, a nested IF ... ELSE statement will be executed, which will then look more closely at the variable called x.

To use IF statements to their best, you will need comparison operators and that is the subject of the next part.

Comparison Operators

Operator	Description	Example	Result
==	Equal to	1 == 1	true
===	Equal in value and type	1 === '1'	false
!=	Not equal to	1 != 2	true
!==	Not equal in value and type	1 !== '1'	true
>	Greater than	1 > 2	false
<	Less than	1 < 2	true
>=	Greater than or equal to	1 >= 1	true
<=	Less than or equal to	2 <= 1	false

So far, our IF statements have looked to see if a condition evaluates true or false and have made use of the double == symbols. There are some other operators that you may use as well and these are called comparison operators. These are the more common ones and all will evaluate to either true or false:

- != Is not equal to
- \> Greater Than
- < Less Than
- \>= Greater Than or equal to
- <= Less Than or equal to
- === The same as and of the same variable type

Let's try them out by changing our code between the JavaScript tags, or you can create a new page if you want:

<SCRIPT LANGUAGE = "Javascript">

var over_twentyone = true;

if (over_twentyone != true) {

document.write("You're not old enough!");

}

else {

document.write("Congratulations - you are old enough!");

}

</SCRIPT>

What this script has done is given the variable named over_twentyone a value of true. We are using an IF ... ELSE statement to see what is in the variable so, in between the round brackets is this:

over_twentyone != true

This is saying "If over_twentyone does not equal True" so if the variable doesn't have what we want we need something else to happen.

However, it does have the true value so JavaScript will jump to the ELSE part of the statement. This gives the text of "Congratulations – you are old enough!) on the browser.

Save and test your work and then change var over_twentyone = true to read var over_twentyone = false. Now save the code and run it again – you will see the message that reads "You're not old enough!"

Have a go at this script:

<SCRIPT LANGUAGE = "Javascript">

var available_width = window.innerWidth;

if (available_width > 800) {

document.write("Show large image");

}

else {

document.write("Show small image");

}

</SCRIPT>

The first line is giving the browser the available Inner Width so we want to see what this is. In the IF statement we are using the Greater Than comparison operator (>) to see if the value in the variable called available width is over 800 pixels. If the value is more than 800 the condition will evaluate to true and a larger image is shown; if it is false, the small image is shown.

Exercise
Reduce your browser size and refresh to see what happens. If you go below 800 in width you should find that the ELSE part is executed.

Exercise
Change > (greater than) to < (less than) and then change the document.write messages so they are correct. What happens now?

The last operator to talk about is the === symbols. These are known as the identity operator and we use this when we want to check equality in a variable and that it is of the same type of variable. Look at this example:

var identity = 27;

if (identity === 27) {

document.write("variable is the number 27");

}

```
else if (identity == 27) {

document.write("variable is the text 27");

}
```

When you run this, the initial IF statement should evaluate true which means that the variable does contain the value of 27 and that it is of a number type. However, if you were to change the initial line to this:

```
var identity = "27";
```

Because we have placed 27 inside quotes, we turned it into a text string so, when we run the code again, the ELSE part will now evaluate true while the first bit evaluates to false.

The === symbol gives you far more precision than the == symbol. Don't worry yourself too much about this though; unless it is absolutely necessary, we will continue to use the == symbol.

In the next part, we will be looking at logical operators.

Logical Operators

```
<!DOCTYPE HTML>
<HTML>
        <HEAD>
        <TITLE>Logical Operators</TITLE>

        <SCRIPT LANGUAGE = "Javascript">

                var cookies_enabled = true;
                var javascript_enabled = false;

                if (cookies_enabled && javascript_enabled) {
                        document.write("ALL OK - continue");
                }
                else {
                        document.write("ALL NOT OK - issue warning.");
                }

        </SCRIPT>

        </HEAD>

        <BODY>

        </BODY>
</HTML>
```

The best operators to use with conditional IF statements are logical operators. These provide you with many more options to use in your IF statements but there are only three that you really need to learn:

- && - Two ampersands mean AND
- || = Two pipe characters mean OR
- ! - One exclamation mark/point means NOT

Let's create this code for a web page. Create a new page or use your template

<!DOCTYPE HTML>

```
<HTML>
<HEAD>
<TITLE>Logical Operators</TITLE>
<SCRIPT LANGUAGE = "Javascript"›
var cookies_enabled = true;
var javascript_enabled = false;
if (cookies_enabled && javascript_enabled) {
document.write( ALL OK - continue");
else [
document.write("ALL IS NOT OK - issue a warning.");
</SCRIPT>
</HEAD>
<BODY>
 </BODY>
</HTML>
```

We start by setting up a pair of Boolean variables:

```
var cookies_enabled = true;
var javascript_enabled = false;
```

Then we want to see what is inside each of the variables so we use the IF statement together with && (two ampersands) in between the round brackets:

if (cookies_enabled && javascript_enabled) {

Note that we have used a shorthand method of checking the Boolean variables:

cookies_enabled && javascript_enabled

When we could have written this:

cookies_enabled == true && javascript_enabled == true

However, when we check a Boolean variable, we can omit the ==true. By doing this, JavaScript will think that you are looking for a true value, which is what you are doing of course. The entire line will read "IF cookies_enabled equals true AND javascript_enabled equals true".

If both of these conditions are true the entire statement that is in between the round brackets will also be true. In this case, the initial document.write is going to be executed. But, if one of the conditions evaluates to false, the entire statement will be false and, in this case, the ELSE part gets executed.

Type in the script and run it. Now edit javascript_enabled = false to read javascript_enabled = true. Save it, refresh and see what happens. You should see the first document.write gets printed.

OR operators (||) are what let you check to see if one value evaluates to true. Edit the IF statement so it looks like this:

if (cookies_enabled || javascript_enabled) {

The entire line will now read " IF cookies_enabled equals true OR javascript_enabled equals true".

On the first line of the code, change cookies_enabled = true to cookies_enabled = false Save the code and run it. You should see that, once again, the initial document.write is printed. Now set both of the variables to false and you will see that the ELSE part gets executed.

So, the OR operators mean that only one bit of an IF statement has to evaluate true and that will make the whole statement true. Let's look at a last example to clear that up a bit more. Edit your script so it reads like this:

var age = 27;

```
if ( age >= 18 && age <= 31 ) {

document.write("Between 18 and 31");

}

else {

document.write("Not Between 18 and 31");

}
```

The script is checking a range of ages. We set a variable named age with a value of 27 and then used an IF statement to check what the contents of the variable are. The following goes between the round brackets:

```
age >= 18 && age <= 31
```

This line says, "IF age is greater than or equal to 18 AND age is less than or equal to 31". If both of these conditions are true, the entire statement is true and we will see the initial document.write executed. If one is false the whole statement will be false. To see that more clearly, change the value of the age variable to 15. Save it and run it in your browser and you should see that the ELSE part of the statement is executed.

Exercise

Add in an ELSE IF statement to check a range of ages between 14 and 17,

The NOT Operator

Above, you saw how we check for a true value using a shorthand method:

if (cookies_enabled && javascript_enabled) {

This means that you do not need to type in cookies_enabled == true. The reason you can do this is that Javascript checks, by default, to see if the Boolean variables have true values. If you wanted to see if there was a false value you would use the NOT operator which is nothing more than an exclamation mark (!). Have a look at this example:

if (!cookies_enabled) {

}

Note that the variable named cookies_enabled now has a NOT operator in front of it. Javascript will check, by default, for a true value and. By putting the NOT operator into the equation, in front of the Boolean value, you are saying "if NOT true" Clearly, if something isn't true then it must be false so, if you are looking for a quicker way of checking for false value types, add an exclamation mark in front of the Boolean variable.

One of the more common uses of the NOT operator is in toggling Booleans to true or false and we do that like this:

bool_value = !bool_value;

On the right-hand side of the = symbol, the NOT operator toggles the value. Once the value has been flipped, Javascript will place the answer in the variable that is on the left of the = symbol. This is exactly the same variable that you will see on the right so bool_value will be opposite to what it was before. In simpler terms, that means that, if the value of the variable called bool_value was true before, it will now be false. Likewise, if it was originally false, it will now be true. Try this code to see it in action:

```
var bool_value = true;
document.write( bool_value + "<BR>" );
bool_value = !bool_value;
document.write( bool_value );
```

You should see that true is written first and then false second. Now edit the first line to read false instead of true and run the script again. Now it should be the other way around — false first and then true.

Don't worry too much if you don't fully understand Boolean flipping. It isn't that important, I just wanted to demonstrate it to you.

Next, we are going to look at switch statements.

Switch Statements

Example:

```
public static void main(String[] args) {

    int user = 18;

    switch ( user ) {
        case 18:
            System.out.println("You're 18");
            break;
      case 19:
            System.out.println("You're 19");
            break;
      case 20:
            System.out.println("You're 20");
            break;
      default:
            System.out.println("You're not 18, 19 or 20");
    }

}
```

On occasion, you will find that you have to check more than a single value for the variables, so for this you can either use several IF ... ELSE statements, which can make your code look a little messy, or you could use a Switch statement. Look at this example:

```
var age = 16;

switch (age) {

case 16:

document.write("under 18");

break;

case 24:

document.write("over 18");

break;

default:

document.write("can't tell");

break;

}
```

What we have done here is set up a variable named age and then we stored a value in it – that value is 16. The switch statement will look at the value to see what it is. If it turns out that age does have a value of 16 in it, the code will be executed. The use of the break keyword is for escaping out of the switch statement – if you omit this, Javascript will just continue down through the statements and assume that all the other cases evaluate true. This will mean all other case code gets executed. If no cases apply then we can add a default value.

Do look carefully at the switch statement syntax. Note that we use lowercase for the word switch and this is then followed by a set of round brackets. Inside these brackets, you will input the name of the variable or the condition that you are testing. This evaluates true or false and that depends on which of the cases match. Javascript examines the case list and attempts to locate a match. If one is found the code is executed. If a match cannot be found, Javascript will execute the default option. Do be aware of the location of the curly brackets and the colons. There is one set of curly brackets for the whole statement and a colon after each of the cases.

All that said, the switch statement is not all that useful in JavaScript because you can't easily test out a range of values if you can at all. If you wanted to check a range of ages, for example, you would want to check something like 16 to 24 or 25 to 60. The switch statement doesn't let you do this so you would need a case for each of the ages and that can add up to a lot of cases. They are useful in a few situations so you do need to be aware of them.

Programming Loops

```
<!DOCTYPE HTML>
<HTML>
        <HEAD>
                <TITLE>For Loops</TITLE>

                <SCRIPT LANGUAGE = "Javascript">

                var answer=0;
                var start_value = 1;
                var end_value = 11;

                for ( start_value; start_value < end_value; start_value++ ) {
                        answer = answer + start_value;

                }

                document.write("answer= " + answer);

                </SCRIPT>
        </HEAD>

        <BODY>

        </BODY>
</HTML>
```

There is one tool that is common to all programming languages – the loop. Usually, programs get executed from top to bottom, each code line being processed in turn. If you wanted to go up rather than down, you would use a loop. These loops are a really good way of executing one or more lines of code over and again. There are a few reasons why you might want to do this but look at the next example:

var total;
total = 11 + 12 + 13 + 14 + 15 + 16 + 17 + 18 + 19 + 20;

All this code does is add the numbers from 11 through to 20 and this is great if you only wanted to add 10 numbers. What if you had

100 numbers that you wanted to add? Or even 1000? You could type them all out if you wanted but it would take a long time and it wouldn't look very pretty. What would you do is use a loop – with this, you can add as many numbers as you want with just a couple of lines of code. The most common loop is the for loop.

For Loops

The for in the for loop is always lowercase and the loop looks like this:

for (start_value; end_value; increment_value)
{

}

The loop always begins with for. This is followed by a space and a set of round brackets. In those brackets you need to have three things, each one separated by a semicolon:

- A starting value for the for loop;
- A way for that loop to end;
- A way of getting from the starting value to the end, known as an increment value

After that we have a set of curly brackets and, inside these, you add the code that you want to be repeatedly executed. Take the following example, which adds the number 12 to 20 and create a web page to try it out:

```
<!DOCTYPE HTML> <HTML>
<HEAD>
<TITLE>For Loops</TITLE>
<SCRIPT LANGUAGE = -Javascript->
var answer=0;
var start_value = 11; var end_value = 20;
for ( start_value; start_value < end_value; start_value++ answer = answer + start_value;
document.write("answer=  + answer);
</SCRIPT>
</HEAD>
<BODY>
</BODY>
<(HTML>
```

What is the first thing you see? We have set up two variables, one each for the start and end values of the loop. A loop is, as you would expect, designed to go around repeatedly for a set number of times. You must tell Javascript how many times. So, you must have a start value and you must have an end value. There

for-loop

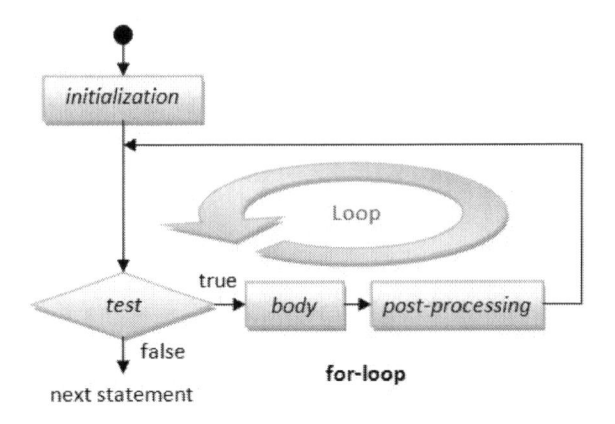

next statement

are a few ways that you can set the end value but what we are saying here is to keep going around until the starting value is more than the end value. How does the for loop know that the starting value is less than the end? Simply because we set the increment value, like this:

start_value++

This is the short way of saying that you want to "add 1 to the start_value variable". This is known as incrementation of a variable – the long way of writing it would be:

start_value = start_value + 1

If you were to carry out the calculation on the right first, the above line would make a lot more sense. Javascript looks at what the start_value variable currently holds and then adds 1. The result is then put into the variable on the left, removing the contents and setting a brand-new value. The result of this is that, on each round of the loop, the variable called start_value will continue to increase by 1.

You can also decrease by 1, like this:

start_value--

A pair of minus signs (--) following the variable is known as the decrement operator and they will take 1 away from the value of the variable. Another way of saying it would be:

start_value = start_value - 1

So, to recap, the starting value of the for loop is the number that we added to the variable called start_value. The ending condition is when the value of start_value is no longer less than the value that we added to the variable called end_value. We get from one to the other by incrementing the variable, start_value:

Let's look closer at what we have in the curly brackets:

answer = answer + start_value;

This is why we use a loop – to run a piece of code repeatedly.

Okay, we want to add the numbers 1 to 10 so, the calculation to the right of the = symbol is carried out first. Javascript looks at the value held in the variable called answer and, first time around the loop the value will be zero. This is because that's how we set it at the start of the code. To get 1, we add 1 to the zero and that is then placed into the variable on the left of the = symbol which, as we now know, is the variable called answer. The contents of the variable will be removed and the new value of 1 stored in its place.

Because we have incremented the variable called start-value and this is incremented in each loop around, the value is going to keep on changing. The second time around, the values will be:

answer	answer	start_value
1	1	2

We added 1 +2 on the right of the = symbol and 3, the answer is then stored in the variable on the left. This means that on the third go around, the values will be

answer   answer   start_value

3   3   3

Remember that the calculations on the right are done first and the result stored in the left

Fourth go around, the values will be:

answer	answer	start _value
6	6	4

Each time around the loop the value of start_value will increase by 1 – we are getting closer to the correct answer! Here's the fifth go around the loop:

answer	answer	start _value
10 =	1Q	5

The last line just writes the answer out. To see better what is happening here, add in the following document.write to the curly brackets in the loop:

answer = answer + start_value;
document.write("answer= " + answer + " start value = " + start_value + "<BR>");

Now, when you run the code, you should see this in your browser:

answer= 1 start value = 1

answer= 3 start value = 2.

answer= 6 start value = 3

answer= 10 start value = 4

answer= 15 start value = 5

answer= 21 start value = 6

answer= 2.8 start value = 7

answer= 36 start value = 8

answer= 45 start value = 9

answer= 55 start value = 10

By the time we get to the end, we should have an answer of 55, after going around the loop 10 times and adding up each time.

Exercise
Print the numbers 1 to 20 using a for loop

Exercise
Print the odd numbers between 1 and 20 using a for loop. You will need to make use of modulus here, as well as an IF statement. The loop should look like:

for (start_value; start_value < end_value; start_value++) {

if ( ) {

document.write("answer= " + start_value + "<BR>");

}

}

It's up to you to fill in what goes in between the curly brackets!

Common End Values

One more common end value for a loop is to find the length of something, perhaps a text string for example, or maybe an array length – more about arrays in the next section. Look at the example below to see how we use length:

```
var start_value = 1;

var some_string = "ABCDEFGH";

for ( start_value; start_value < some_string.length; start_value++ ) {

}
```

Length method can be used by all strings and it will tell you the number of characters in a string of text. We loop around for as long as the start value remains below the length of the string called some_string but, when the value goes above the string length, the loop comes to an end.

Don't worry too much about these because, as we come up against them, I will explain them to you.

while loops

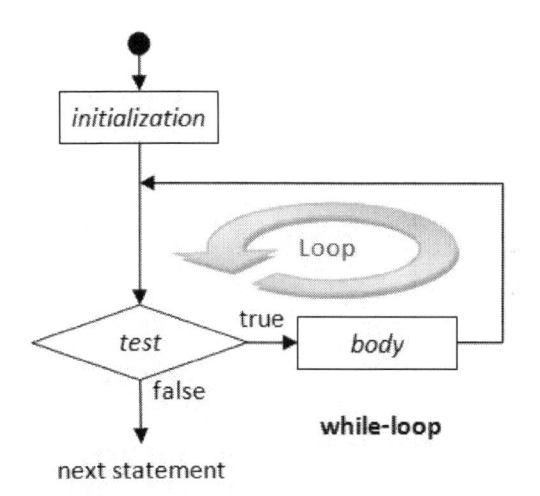

next statement

while-loop

The while in the while loop always begins with a lowercase w and these are another great tool for you to learn. This is what the while loop looks like:

while (condition_to_test) {

}

Rather than using the word 'for', we use the word 'while'. This is followed by a space and then a set of round brackets. In these brackets, we have a condition that we want to test and this will evaluate true or false. While the condition evaluates true, the loop will continue to go around. When it evaluates false, the loop will stop. Look at the following example:

```
var counter = 1;
var answer = 0;

while (counter < 11) {

answer = answer + counter;
counter++;

}

document.write("answer= " + answer);
```

We have got two variables here – one named counter and one named answer, just like in a previous example. In the round brackets, we have:

counter < 11

Each time the loop goes around, it will evaluate to true or to false. It is saying, 'while counter is less than 11 keep looping"

In order for a code to be executed, you need to have a set of curly brackets and this is what goes inside those:

```
answer = answer + counter;
counter++;
```

Again, we are adding the numbers from 1 to 10, the same as we did earlier. However, this time, we want to add the value that is contained in the variable called answer and the variable called counter. The counter variable must move on by 1 every time the loop goes around otherwise we would have an infinite loop, one that never ends. Line 2 will increment that variable:

counter++;

On the second go around the loop, the variable called counter is 2 and, as that is lower than 11, the loop will continue. When that gets to 11, the condition inside the round brackets will evaluate false and the loop ends.

The while loop is a good deal easier to get the hang of than a for loop and the one you use will depend entirely on the situation. Learn both though, it will serve you well Have a go at these exercises:

Exercise
Add the numbers from 1 to 20 using the while loop

Exercise
Print the even numbers between 1 and 20 using

a while loop. You will need modulus and an IF statement for this.

In the next section, we are moving on to look at arrays.

Section 5: Arrays and Functions

Arrays

```
<!DOCTYPE HTML>
<HTML>
        <HEAD>
                <TITLE>Simple Array</TITLE>
                <SCRIPT LANGUAGE = "Javascript">
                        var my_array = [10, "ten", true];
                        document.write( my_array[0] );
                </SCRIPT>
        </HEAD>

        <BODY>

        </BODY>
</HTML>
```

Normal variables in JavaScript hold just one piece of data but, if you wanted to hold more data in the same name, you would use an array. There are several ways to set your array up but by far the easiest is this way:

var my_array = [10, "ten", true];

this is an array that holds three separate values under one variable that we named my_array. Note that you can store different data types in an array – Booleans, numbers and text strings.

Each value must be separated by a comma and must be enclosed in square brackets that follow an = symbol.

To access all your values, you need to use an index value. This is indicated by a number in between a set of square brackets and that number will correspond to the position of a specific value in the array. One thing to remember is that positions in a JavaScript index start at 0:

my_array[0]
my_array[1]
my_array[2]

Therefore, my_array[0] holds a number value of 10, my_array[1] has the text value of 'ten' and my_array[2] has the Boolean value of true. It would then be easy to write those values to a web page, like this:

document.write(my_array[0] + "<BR>");
document.write(my_array[1] + "<BR>");
document.write(my_array[2] + "<BR>");

Try the following script to test this out:

<!DOCTYPE HT L>

<HTML>

```
<HEAD>
<TITLE>Simple Array</TITLE>
<SCRIPT LANGUAGE = "Javascript">
var my_array = [10, "ten", true];
document.write( my_array[0] ); </SCRIPT>
</HEAD>
<BODY>
</BODY>
</HTML>
```

Save your work and run it in your browser; you should see the number 10 on your screen. Now edit the position value of 0, between the square brackets, to read 1. Save and refresh the page and now you will see the word "ten" displayed on the screen. Change it to a 2 and the value of true will be displayed on the screen.

Now edit that 2 into a 3 – you will now see the word "undefined" on the screen. This is because your array only has three items in it. By typing a 3, you are trying to access the 4th item in the array and that doesn't exist – remember, positions begin at zero so your three items are positions 0, 1, 2. However, rather than kicking up an error, like other programming languages would, and rather than just not working, JavaScript will add the new position at the end of your array as undefined. You can store data in this new position as well. Edit your script so it reads like this - :

var my_array = [10, "ten", true];

document.write(my_array[3] + "<BR>");

my_array[3] ="new item";

document.write(my_array[3]);

Now JavaScript will print "undefined" first and then it will print "new item".

Note how we have assigned a new value:

my_array[3] ="new item";

To the left of the = symbol, we have got the array name followed by a set of square brackets. In those brackets, we have the number of the array position that we want to access. Following the = symbol is the value that you want to be assigned. So, it is similar to the way we normally assign values to variables except for the addition of the square brackets and the position number of the array after the name of the variable.

There is also another way of setting up an array and that is using the new keyword:

var my_array = new Array( );

This time, note that the word new and then a space now follows the = symbol. The word "Array" follows that, (always a capital A, never lowercase) and this is immediately followed by a set of round brackets. Inside these you can insert the number of positions that will be in the array if you want:

var my_array = new Array(3);

What this code is saying is that we want to set up an array that has three positions but you are not obliged to add in the number of positions if you don't want to. However, when you do assign a value to each position, you must add in the index position, like this:

var my_array = new Array( );
my_array[0] = 10;
my_array[1] = "ten";
my_array[2] = true;

The top line is setting up the array with the name of my_array. The following three lines then assign a value to each of the positions that are in the array and this is the method we are going to use from now on when we set arrays up.

Arrays and Loops

Very often, you will use arrays and loops together and the reason for this is that the array index positions are numbers that can be swapped for loop variables. Try the following code to see how this works:

```
var counter = 0;
var lottery_numbers = new Array();

while ( counter < 49 ) {

lottery_numbers[counter] = counter + 1;
document.write( lottery_numbers[counter] + "<BR>" );
counter++;

}
```

What this script is doing is assigning values to the lottery_numbers array using a while loop. This loop continues to go around, executing this line repeatedly:

```
lottery_numbers[counter] = counter + 1;
```

Instead of using the index positions and having to write each one out individually, like lottery_numbers[0], lottery_numbers[1], etc., instead we put the counter variable in place of the index number. The reason we can do this is that counter will change with every loop around and JavaScript is already aware of what is in counter; thus, it can be used as the index. After the = symbol, we can assign the value of the counter variable (plus 1) to each of the array positions.

There is so much more that you can do with arrays and you will come across them again later. For now, we need to move on and talk about functions

Functions

Right now, the scripts we are using have been set so that they run the minute the page loads up in the browser but this isn't necessary. Perhaps a better way would be to place the JavaScript code into a function. These are nothing more than additional segments of code that may be called into action. In fact, unless you call a specific function into action, it won't do anything at all. Let's have a look at how they work.

A function that does not include any code will look like this:

```
function myFunction() {

}
```

The word 'function' (with a lowercase f) is followed by a space. Then you add the name that you have chosen for your function. These are very similar to variables in that they may be named anything but cannot start with a number, cannot have any spaces in the name and should only contain numbers, letters, underscores and $ signs.

This is followed by a set of round brackets and in these, we will add something called arguments. We will come to those later but next is set of curly brackets and that is where your code goes. There is no need for you to have your functions spread out over several lines, you can do this if you want:

```
function myFunction() { alert("My Function");
}
```

However, for the sake of clarity and readability, it is better to spread the functions out.

Create a new page and on between your script tags, input the following code:

```
function myFunction( ) {

alert( "My Function" );

}
```

Your code should look something like this:

```
<!DOCTYPE HTML>

<HTML>

<HEAD>

<TITLE>-A Simple Function</TITLE>

<SCRIPT LANGUAGE = "Javascript">
```

```
function myFunction() {
alert("my Function");
</SCRIPT>
</HEAD>
<BODY>
</BODY>
</HTML>
```

Save your code and load the page into the web browser. If nothing happens, then you did it right because the code that is between the curly brackets does not display. Why? Because we didn't call that function into action – remember, when a function isn't called into action it doesn't do anything.

There are several ways to call functions into action and one of those is through onLoad – an event of the browser window. Add this code to the BODY section of your script:

```
<BODY onLoad = "myFunction()">
```

After onLoad, there is an = symbol and after this, we have the name of the function that was created – this is the function that we want to call into action. It is best to put this function name in between a set of double or single quotes because some browsers won't react unless those quotes are in place. You will also need a set of round brackets.

Save the changes and load the page into the browser; you should now see an alert box on the screen – this tells you that the function has now been called into action

Functions That Call Other Functions

It is also possible for a function to call another function into action. You really don't want one huge function that does it all so the best way is to have several smaller functions that each do something specific. Let's say that you have a function that extracts values from a form whenever a button gets clicked. You could then set up more functions that check, perhaps an email box to see if an input email is valid or that a checkbox has been correctly ticked. The point I am making is that it is much easier for you and for anyone who reads your code if you break it down into smaller, more manageable chunks that each does a specific job.

Have a look at this simple example – one function is calling another function:

<!DOCTYPE HTML> <HTML>

<HEAD>

<TITLE>A simple Function</TITLE>

<SCRIPT LANGUAGE = "Javascript"› function myFunction()

secondFunction();

1

function secondFunction()

alert("my second Function");

</SCRIPT>

</HEAD>

-BODY onload = "myFunction()"›

</BODY>

</HTML>

We added another function to the code we wrote earlier – this is it:

function secondFunction() {

alert("My Second Function");

}

The code that is in between the curly brackets for the function is only an alert box. Let's look at the first function:

function myFunction() {

secondFunction();

}

Now we don't have the alert box in the first function but what we do have is this:

secondFunction();

So, when you want to call a function into action, all you do is input the name of the function, add in the round brackets and then end with the semicolon.

Have a go for yourself. When you load up the page into a browser, the first thing that happens is the onLoad call in the BODY. This will then activate myFunction and when this is executed, it will then call secondFunction into action.

Return Values

```
// A function can return value of any type using the
// keyword "return".

// The same function can possibly return values
// of different types
function foo (p1) {
    if (typeof(p1) == "number")
        return 0;    // Return a number
    else
    if (typeof(p1) == "string")
        return "zero"; // Return a string

    // If no value being explicitly returned
    // "undefined" is returned.
}

foo(1);           // returns 0
foo("abc");       // returns "zero"
foo();            // returns undefined
```

Sometimes you are going to want something back from those functions. Let's say that you are checking an email address to see if there are any errors in it; you will want the results from your code – is it valid or not? Or maybe you have a checkbox that asks a user to agree to the terms and conditions of your website – again, you want a result back. This is a value that we call the return value and this can be of a numerical value, a Boolean, a text string, even an object. However, there will only be one return value.

Let's edit secondFunction so that it will return a value:

function secondFunction() {

var alertString = "My Return Value";

return alertString;

}

In this example, we created a variable that we called alertString. We set the value of this as a text string that reads, "My Return Value" and, to get the value from the function, we use this line:

return alertString;

To retrieve a value all you do is input the word, 'return' and follow it with a space. Next comes the name of the variable or the value that you want. In our case, we used the variable name alertString.

We do need to make a change to firstFunction so that we can access the return value. Have a look at this:

function myFunction() {

var retVal = secondFunction();

alert(retVal);

}

The important part of this code is:

var retVal = secondFunction();

We have still got a function call but we have placed to the right of the = symbol. Remember that a single = symbol is the assignment operator so we have assigned a value to the variable that is on the left. The value we assign to this variable will be the value that comes back from secondFunction. So, keep in mind that, to get a value returned from the function, we need to assign it to a variable that is on the left side of the = symbol.

Next, we are looking at function arguments.

Function Arguments

```
function myFunction() {
        var cookiesEnabled = window.navigator.cookieEnabled;
        var retVal = secondFunction( cookiesEnabled );
        alert( retVal );
}

function secondFunction( cookiesEnabled ) {
        var alertString;
        if ( cookiesEnabled == true) {
                alertString = "Cookies Enabled";
        }
        else {
                alertString = "Cookies Not Enabled";
        }
        return alertString;
}
```

Values can be passed to a function and these values are known as arguments. Arguments are placed within the round brackets that go with the function. If there is more than one value that needs to be passed over, just make sure they are separated by commas. Have a look at this example, a piece of new code that shows you how to use arguments:

function myFunction()

var cookiesEnabled = window.navigatorcookieEnabled; var retVal = secondFunction(cookiesEnabled);

alert(retVal);

function secondFunction(cookiesEnabled) var alertString;

if(cookiesEnabled == true) {

alert tying = "Cookies Enabled";

else (

alertString = "Cookies Not Enabled";

return al et-15th ng;

So, in this function, we have a new variable that we called cookiesEnabled:

var cookiesEnabled = window.navigator.cookieEnabled;

What we want to do is see if a user has got cookies enabled in their browser so, our second code line is:

var retVal = secondFunction(cookiesEnabled);

Between the round brackets of the function call, we have input our new variable called cookiesEnabled. This is going to evaluate true or false, depending on the settings on the user's browser. By inputting the name of a variable in the function call brackets, we have set an argument but you can also use values, such as text strings, numbers or Booleans as well as variable names.

So, the value of cookiesEnabled will be passed to secondFunction but take a look at how we have now laid out secondFunction:

function secondFunction(cookiesEnabled) {

Note that we also have a variable name in between the round brackets for secondFunction as well, the same variable as we had for myFunction. It doesn't need to be the same; you can use whatever name you like, for example:

var retVal = secondFunction(cookiesEnabled);

function secondFunction(cookiesEnabled_two) {

The result is going to be the same; no matter what is in the variable that is in the calling function, it will be passed to the function that has been called. You could do this if you wanted:

```
var retVal = secondFunction( true );

function secondFunction( cookiesEnabled ) {
```

Now the function call has been given a value of true, hard-coded between the brackets so this means that the value of true is going to be put into the variable called cookiesEnabled.

The code that we used in secondFunction makes use of an IF statement to see if cookiesEnabled evaluates true or false. Then, it will return a string value. If you wanted, you could make the code even simpler, like this:

```
function secondFunction( cookiesEnabled )

if ( cookiesEnabled == true) (

return "Cookies Enabled";

else {

return "Cookies Not Enabled";

}
```

This time, we left out the variable called alertString and, instead, we now have two return uses; the first is for the IF bit and the second for the ELSE bit. JavaScript sees the keyword return as a STOP sign – once the return line has been executed, JavaScript will get out of the function and will not execute any of the code that comes after it.

It is possible to pass more than one value to a function. Look at the code below where secondFunction has been set up with two arguments placed between the round brackets:

function secondFunction(cookiesEnabled, isOnline){ if(cookiesEnabled && isOnline)

return "All OK";

else (

return "Cookies not enabled or not online";

Each of the arguments is separated by a comma. Now, when we need to call the function, we may use both of the arguments:

function myFunction()

var cookiesEnabled = window.navigator.cookieEnabled; var isOnline = window.navigator.onLine;

var retVal = secondFunction(cookiesEnabled, isOnline); alert(retVal);

Our arguments are being passed over in this way:

```
var retVal = secondFunction( cookiesEnabled, isOnline );
```

So, whatever values are in the variables will automatically be passed to the variables that are in secondFunction. However, in JavaScript, there is no need to pass the same number of arguments. You could do this:

```
var retVal = secondFunction( cookiesEnabled );
```

We only passed one argument here, one of the values that were set up by secondFunction. Unlike other languages, JavaScript doesn't give you any error messages if the number of arguments doesn't agree. If you wanted, you could omit both of the arguments between the brackets and JavaScript won't bat an eyelid. So, this next example would also be valid, if a little pointless:

```
var retVal = secondFunction();
```

In this secondFunction code, ELSE will be executed but, in practice, you really want the number of arguments to be matching. So, if you have a function that accepts two arguments then the line that calls the function should pass two values over otherwise it can get somewhat confusing.

Next, we are going to discuss variable scope.

Variable Scope

```
<!DOCTYPE HTML>
<HTML>
    <HEAD>
        <TITLE>Text Box Checker</TITLE>
        <SCRIPT LANGUAGE = "Javascript">

            function validate() {
                var textbox_value = document.getElementById("Name").value;
                if (textbox_value == "") {
                    var error = "<span STYLE=color:red>Required</span>";
                    document.getElementById("message").innerHTML = error
                    return false;
                }
                else {
                    document.getElementById("message").innerHTML ="First Name";
                }
            }
        </SCRIPT>
    </HEAD>
    <BODY>

        <P ID="message">First Name</P>

        <INPUT TYPE ="text" SIZE="25" VALUE="" ID="Name">
        <INPUT TYPE ="button" value ="  SUBMIT  " onclick = "validate()">
    </BODY>
</HTML>
```

All variables, no matter what programming language you are using, have a scope and this is all about where that variable may be seen from. Any variable that has been declared inside a function with the var keyword may not be seen from outside of the function. Have a look at this code:

```
function myFunction() {

var alertString = "ALERT!!!";
secondFunction();

}

function secondFunction() {

alert( alertString );

}
```

Our first function has got a variable set inside the curly brackets and this is named alertString. Note that we used the var keyword to set this up. Our second function is using an alertbox to try to access the function but the code won't work. Instead, you see an error message that says "alertString is not defined" the reason it won't work is because that particular variable, the one named alertString, is a local variable, local to myFunction. That is because it was set up using the var keyword inside the function and the second function cannot see it.

To change this, we can make our variables into global variables. To do this, you simply declare the variable outside the functions, just like this:

```
var alertString = "ALERT!";
```

```
function myFunction() {
secondFunction();
}
function secondFunction() {
alert( alertString );
}
```

Now that the variable has been declared externally to the functions, the code now works. Another way to achieve this is to simply omit the keyword var from the variable. However, JavaScript scope can be a little complex, especially when we consider prototypes and closure. So, rather than burying you in a mire of information, we're going to leave it there - this is for beginners, after all. All you need to remember is that, when you declare a variable inside a function, you must take care – if you use the var keyword, that variable cannot be seen outside of the function.

To finish off this section, we will look at a bit of code that makes use of functions within a real-life setting. Look at the code below – the code that is in the BODY section is setting up a button and a text box. We want out users to input something into the box so if, when the button gets clicked, that box is empty, an error message will be displayed to the user. This is the code:

<!DOCTYPE HTML

<HEAD>

```
<TITLE,-Text Box Checker./TITLE› <SCRIPT LANGUAGE - "javascript" function validate() (

vat textbox_value = document.getElementById("Name"),value:

if (textbox_value =="")

var error - -<span STYLE-color:red-Required<span-"; document.getElementById("message").innerHTML . error return false;

else {

document.getElementByld("message-),InnerHTML -"First Name";

</SCRIPT>

</HEAD>

<BODY>

<P ID="message"›First Name</P›

<INPUT TYPE ="text" Size="25" VALUE= ID-"Name"),

-INPUT TYPE -"button- value 4" SUBMIT - onclick - "validate()"›

</BODY>
```

The code in the BODY is:

```
<P ID="message">First Name</P>
<INPUT TYPE ="text" SIZE="25" VALUE="" ID="Name">
<INPUT TYPE ="button" value =" SUBMIT " onClick = "validate()">
```

The first line is simply a pair of paragraph tags containing the text "First Name" and the P tag also contains an ID and this ID is what is being used in the JavaScript.

The second and third lines are the tags for the button and text box; the box also has an ID. When the button gets clicked, it will call the function validate that is in between the script tags in HEAD:

onClick = "validate()"

The first line of the validate function code is:

var textbox_value = document.getElementById("Name").value;

We set up a variable with a name of textbox_value and we want to store the textbox value in it. We do this through the getElementById property from the document object. In between the round brackets is the text box ID and, following the dot, is the value.

This is sufficient information to retrieve a VALUE attribute from that text box.

Now we will want to test the contents of the box so, to do this, we use an IF ... ELSE statement. The IF bit is:

```
if (textbox_value == "") {

var error = "<span STYLE=color:red>Required</span>";
document.getElementById("message").innerHTML = error;

}
```

All that is stored in the error variable is some CSS and HTML:

```
"<span STYLE=color:red>Required</span>";
```

We used a SPAN tag and applied a style to it. This will make the test "Required" to be colored in red. Next, we have this line:

```
document.getElementById("message").innerHTML = error;
```

What this does is sets text in HTML. The paragraph tag ID was message and can use this together with document.getElementByID. Did you spot that we had an innerHTML bit after the dot? This lets you set text in the HTML and the inner is the bits between the P tags:

<P ID="message">First Name</P>

This is First Name and this will be replaced with new text which will follow the =. In this case, that text will be the value of the variable called error.

ELSE is what sets innerHTML to 'First Name"; not really required but we included it purely for testing.

We also don't really need to return false line but you would use it if your form data were being sent somewhere. This cancels the sending, giving the user the option of trying again.

Exercise

Try the code above for yourself. Typing it gives you practice at setting up both JavaScript and HTML. Clicking the button should display the new text colored red so type in some text and click on the button again – now you should see "First Name" appear.

For the purposes of this book, this is sufficient information on functions, for now. However, you should be aware that you can do so much more with them, such as creating function expressions and self-invoking functions. For now, don't worry about these as they are covered in intermediate to advanced JavaScript.

Section 6: String Manipulation

```
scala> object concat {
     |     def main(args: Array[String]) {
     |     var str1 = "String concatenation can be ";
     |   var str2 = "done using concat method";
     |     var st = str1.concat(str2)
     |     println( "Concatenated String is : " + st );
     |     }
     | }
defined object concat

scala> concat.main(null)
Concatenated String is : String concatenation can be done using concat method

scala>
```

Strings - Changing Case

One of the biggest parts of your JavaScript programming career will be the manipulation of text strings. To give you a helping hand, JavaScript already has plenty of built-in methods for your use and we will be taking a look at these over the course of this section. However, before we go much further, I want you to create a brand-new page containing a pair of SCRIPT tags placed in the HEAD section.

Changing Case

Sometimes, you may want to make a change to the case of a text string so, to do this, there are two built-in methods you can choose from – toUpperCase and toLowerCase. Both are self-explanatory and both are simple to use. Input the following text in between your SCRIPT tags

```
<SCRIPT LANGUAGE = "Javascript">

var postcode = "sr2 4jh";
var new_postcode = postcode.toUpperCase();

document.write( new_postcode );

</SCRIPT>
```

In the first line, you can see that we have set up a new variable that we named postcode. Now, let's say that the value came from a text box that was on a form. You need to ensure that all the letters in the postcode are in UPPERCASE and, to do that, you can use toUpperCase to convert them. This is how you do it:

```
var new_postcode = postcode.toUpperCase();
```

On the right-hand side of the = symbol, you input the name of the variable that you want to convert. Then you have a dot and that is followed by the name of the method which is toUpperCase. This is then followed with the set of round brackets and the line ends, as usual, with the semicolon.

Look to the left of the = symbol. Did you spot a new variable? When the conversion takes place, the new value will go into this variable which we have named new_postcode. There is a good reason why we store this new value in a brand-new variable – JavaScript strings are what we call immutable. This means that nothing can be changed, no characters in the string can be altered in any way. JavaScript comes up with a brand-new string and leaves the original one as it was.

Add a new document.write at the end of the code and also add a BR tag to the first document.write:

document.write(new_postcode + "<BR>");
document.write(postcode);

Save your code and run it in your browser. You should see new_postcode as SR2 5JH while the original, untouched postcode is sr2 4jh.

That said, you can also do this:

```
var postcode = "sr2 4jh";
postcode = postcode.toUpperCase();
```

However, what you are doing here is making a new string on the right of the = symbol and then storing it in the variable called postcode.

Exercise

Edit the variable called postcode on line 1 of the code to SR2 4JH. Now convert it using toLowerCase.

Next, we are going to look at another string method called indexOf.

Strings - indexOf

This method is used to let you know if there is a specific character in a text string, such as @ included in an email address. The one thing it will not do is look for all occurrences of the character, just the initial one and, if it can't locate the character it will return -1 as a value. If it does find the character, the returned value will be the position the character is in the string, for example, 4th character.

Create a new page or edit your code to the following so that we can test indexOf out:

var email = "meme@meme.com";
var at_sign = email.indexOf('@');
document.write(at_sign);

What we have done here is set up a variable that will hold the value of an email address. We need to see there is a @ sign in the email address so we use indexOf in this way:

var at_sign = email.indexOf('@');

Once again, you begin to the right of the = symbol and input the name of the variable you want to look in. A dot follows that and then you have indexOf. The round brackets contain the character/s that you want to find and these must be inserted in between quotation marks. You are not limited to checking for a single character but, if you check for multiple characters the returned result will be the initial character of the string.

When you run the following script, you will see a value of 4 returned. You could be forgiven for believing that the @ symbol in the address is actually at position 5 but, remember, JavaScript indexing begins at 0.

Remove the @ symbol from the address on the first code line and run the script again – a value of -1 should be returned. This information may be used within an IF statement in this way:

if (at_sign == -1) {

document.write("no @ sign in email address");

}

else {

document.write("email address contains @ sign");

}

This code only checks the variable called at_sign for a -1 value and will take the appropriate action. Add this to your code and test it. Then replace the @ sign and run the code again.

The next string method we look at is called charAt.

Strings - charAt

So, previously we looked at how indexOf is used to find where a text string is inside another text string but you could ask for the character, rather than the position number, to be returned as the value instead. To do this, we use the string method called charAt, like this:

if (at_sign == -1) {

document.write("no @ sign in email address");

}
else {

var character = email.charAt(at_sign);
document.write(character);

}

The beginning line of our ELSE section in the IF statement is this:

var character = email.charAt(at_sign);

charAt follows the variable called email and there must be a number inserted between the round brackets. This number is the string position that you want. In our example, the variable called at_sign contained a value of 4, the position of the @ sign in the address and this character then gets stored in the variable named character.

If you wanted the keyboard code of that character then, instead of charAt, you would use charCodeAt, like this:

var character = email.charCodeAt(at_sign);

Now the variable called character will have a value of whatever the keyboard code is on your system – for example, a UK keyboard would return a value of 64.

Next, we look at using a string method called substr to grab characters from text strings.

Strings - substr

You might want to get characters out of a string sometimes. For example, you could get the last 4 characters from an email address to see if it ends with .com. To do this, we use the string method called substr.

For the substr method to work, there must be a minimum of 1 character inserted between the set of round brackets. This number is the position at which you want the search to start. You could also add another number, separated by a comma if you wanted but this is not mandatory. If you do include a second number, however, JavaScript will get all the characters from the start position specified to the end of that string.

Have a look at this code example:

var email = "meme@meme.com";
var ending = email.substr(0, 4);
document.write(ending);

Here, we are grabbing 4 characters from the specified email address and we start the search at position 0 – the first character. If you omit the comma and the second number but retain

0, the substr method will return a value of the entire email address.

You can use a negative number if you want to start the grab at the end of the string. -4, for example, would mean you want the last 4 characters from the end of the specified string. Look at this example:

var email = "meme@meme.com";
var ending = email.substr(-4);
document.write(ending);

This will get you the final 4 characters which, in this case, are .com. Previously, we looked for the @ symbol in the email address but what would happen if the user input more than one @ symbol as a way of trying to trick you? Using indexOf will only tell you where the first occurrence is and will stop when it finds the first one. If you use a loop, together with an IF statement and combine it with substr, you can find all the occurrences of the @ symbol in that email address. Look at this example:

var at_sign = "@meme@meme@.com@";
var counter = 0;
var i;

for (i=0; i < at_sign.length; i++) {

var char = at_sign.substr(i, 1);

```
if (char == "@" ) {

counter++;

}
}
```

document.write("number of times @ appears is: " + counter);

The email address has been set to contain 4 of the @ symbols. Then, we set two variables – on was a counter and the other a loop variable named i. All of the strings contain a property called length – the number of characters in the string. This is what the first line in the for loop would look like:

```
for ( i=0; i < at_sign.length; i++ ) {
```

We continue to loop until the variable called i is not less than the email address length that is stored in the variable called at sign. Each loop increases the value of the i variable by 1 and we can use that when we write our substr method:

```
var char = at_sign.substr( i, 1 );
```

On the first loop, i has a 0 value so substr will read substr(0,1). This tells JavaScript to begin at the first character and get 1 character. N the next loop, the variable will contain a value of 1 so substr reads substr(1,1). It will begin at character 2 and grab 1 character. This continues, grabbing a single character each loop using substr. The IF statement will keep checking to see f that character is an @ symbol – if it is, 1 is added to counter.

So, if you need to check all the characters in your string you need to use substr method.

Finally, we will look at Split and Join.

Strings - Split and Join

Lastly, if you wanted to split up a text string, you would use the split method. Inside the round brackets of the method, you could include a delimiter but this is optional. The delimiter indicated how each part of the slit string will be separated and it could be a comma, space, semicolon, etc. If you use a delimiter, it must be specified between quotation marks and, when a string is split up, it becomes an array. Here's an example:

var email = "me@email_1.com, him@email_2.com, her@email_3.com";
var email_array = email.split(',');

The top line is nothing more than a list of email addresses, each separated by a comma. On the next line, we have the split method. Now look at what comes after the = sign:

email.split(',')

What we are doing is splitting the email variable. Inserted into the round brackets that go with a split is a pair of quote marks with a comma in between. Split searches the string to find commas and will put anything that comes before a comma into a position in an array. Once it is complete, we will have an array that we call email_array. Look at the for loop that will print out each of the email addresses:

var i;

for (i=0; i < email_array.length; i++) {

document.write(email_array[i] + "<BR>");

}

The for loop will continue to go around all the time the variable called i is less than the array length.

Join Method

Text strings can be joined together using the join method. Let's say that we want to separate the email addresses using hyphens and not commas; we would do it like this:

var email = "meme@email_1.com,him@email_2.com,her@email_3.com";
var email_array = email.split(',');
var new_string = email_array.join('-');
document.write(new_string);

Lines 1 and 2 are the same as before but look at line 3:

```
var new_string = email_array.join('-');
```

The join method also makes use of the round brackets with a delimiter, in this case, a hyphen. Now, all the email_array positions will be joined with hyphens.

Again, the join method uses a pair of round brackets with a delimiter inside of them. Each position in the email_array will now be joined together with hyphens.

To have no spaces between the strings, simply omit the delimiter and just have the pair of quote marks on their own.

It will take a lot of skill to master the string methods properly but you do need to learn them. So, have a go with these two exercises for a bit of practice.

Exercise - split
These books have numbers included in the titles:

Catch 22
Slaughterhouse 5
Fahrenheit 451

Write a code that will print only the numbers. Use loops, arrays, and split to come up with a solution.

Exercise - substr

If a user were looking at your website using an iPad, you might see this on the user agent, or something like it:

"Mozilla/5.0(iPad; CPU OS 5_0_1 like Mac OS X)"

Write a code that extracts Mac OS and iPad out of the string. Use two instances of substr and then print the return on a single line using document.write.

Section 7: How JavaScript Works with HTML and CSS

Programming is akin to puzzle solving. In human languages, that puzzle may well to be to translate perfectly into a sentence while, in programming, that puzzle could be to make your web page look a specific way or it could make a page object move, for example.

When web designers are asked to create web pages that are laid out and designed in a specified manner, the designer must take the idea and break it down into smaller pieces and then each piece must be translated into something that the computer may understand – and that means all the instructions must be placed in the right order and use the right syntax.

Each page of a website is built using a series of instructions, separate ones for each bit and all in the right order. The browser, whichever one it is, is one of the biggest players in the code translation, turning it into something that we can easily view on our screens and, in some cases, interact with. It is so easy to forget that your code is nothing more than a text file if it doesn't have a browser it is only when the text is placed into the browser that the real magic can happen. When a user opens the web page, the browser will get the HTML and any other programming language needed and interpret them.

Technically, CSS and HTML are nor programming languages; they are style information (CSS) and page structure (HTML). However, before you can truly understand JavaScript, you do need to understand the basics of CSS and HTML – these are the front end of all applications and web pages.

Early in the 1990's, the only web language available was HTML. Each website was coded, page by page and it was a long job. Thankfully, a good deal has moved on since then and now there is a choice of programming languages to use. We are only interested in JavaScript together with CSS and HTML.

An Overview

HTML is used for the basics of structuring a website and we then use CSS and JavaScript to modify and enhance it:

- CSS controls the layout, formatting and overall presentation
- JavaScript controls how all the different elements behave

Let's look in more detail at each of them so that you can understand how each one fits into making a website work. We'll start with HTML:

HTML

This is the core of every website that you see, no matter how complex it is or how many different technologies are involved. It is one of the most vital skills that any web designer should learn and is the proper starting point if you are looking to learn how to create web content. It is also very easy to learn.

HTML means Hypertext Markup Language. The 'markup' bit means that HTML isn't just a language that uses another language to perform a function; it also identifies content using tags. Think of it this way; take a typical article and label up the page contents. You would most likely come up with a header, a subheader, the text body and maybe a few images with more text at the bottom of the page.

A markup language, like HTML, works the same way except, instead of using text to label the sections, it uses code. More specifically, it uses HTML tags which are also called elements. The names of the tags are quite intuitive – Header tags, Image tags, Paragraph tags, and such like.

Each website has several of these tags, each denoting what type of content is on the page. The content is wrapped up in the relevant tag. For example, what you are reading now is all part of a paragraph. If were coding this a web page the paragraph would have begun with a paragraph tag - <p>. The open brackets denote the tag and the letter tells the computer that this is a paragraph and not another content type.

When a tag is opened, the content that comes after is assumed to be included with the tag, until the tag is closed. When the paragraph is finished, you would have a closing tag </p>. This looks the same as the opening tag but for the addition of the backslash. Have a look at this example:

<p>This would be a paragraph.</p>

With HTML, you can add in headings, make lists, control the line breaks, format your paragraphs, emphasize the text, insert an image, build a table, control the styling, create some special characters and a whole lot more besides.

CSS

Where HTML makes up the structure of the website, CSS is where the styling comes in. The colors, the wonderful fonts, the background and the animations are all down to CSS. It is what sets the tone and this is what makes CSS very powerful and an incredibly powerful tool for any web designer to learn. CSS is also what makes a website adapt to the different sizes of screen and all the different types of device.

While I can't show you what CSS can do, I can ask you to use your imagination. I want you to imagine a web page – first in plain HTML and second, with lots of colors and fancy texts, a nice background image, in CSS and HTML.

On the HTML-only page, you will have all the content but no styling, just plain text. The once looking one you have the text and all the styling and that, if you can imagine it, is the difference.

In simple terms, CSS is nothing more than a series of rules that are used to assign properties to tags – specified for single or multiple tags, a whole document or several documents. The reason why we have CSS is that, as we have evolved with text fonts and different colors, designers have struggled to keep HTML fully adapted.

When HTML was developed, it wasn't designed as a way of showing information about physical formatting. It was only designed as a way of structuring the content of a web document, like paragraphs versus headers. Because HTML couldn't keep up with all the new features in design, CSS was finally developed in 1996. From them on, we could remove all the formatting out of our HTML documents and store it in CSS files separately.

CSS stands for Cascading Style Sheets and the words 'style sheet' is a reference to the actual document. All web browsers have their own default style sheet so every single website uses at least one of these – that will likely be the default for the browser a user access the website through, irrespective of whether any additions or changes have been made by the designer.

Where the word 'cascading' comes into it is this. Most web designers and developers start out with a style sheet that has default styles on it and these will override any browser defaults using custom CSS. Think of a waterfall, picture the water cascading down, hitting all the rocks as it goes down. It is only the last rock it hits that affects where it flows and it is the same with CSS – the final style sheet defined is what tells the browser the important instructions.

JavaScript

Out of all three, JavaScript is the most complicated and the first beta format wasn't released until 1995. These days, all the modern browsers include support for JavaScript and just about every website on the internet today uses it for more complex and powerful functionality.

In short, it is a programming language that allows developers to design websites that are interactive. If you see dynamic behavior on any web page, there's a pretty good bet it's down to JavaScript, a language that boosts the default behaviors and controls of a browser.

One simple example of JavaScript is any popup box that you see on your screen. When you last input some information into a form online and you got a confirmation box pop up on your screen; it might have had a couple of buttons on it, perhaps "OK" and "Cancel. That was all down to JavaScript. As you know from what you already covered in this book, you can use an IF ... ELSE statement in the code that tells the computer to do something if a user clicks one button on the box and something else if the other button is clicked.

Think about a website where you could scroll past the end of the sidebar. This is called a slide-in-call-to-action and JavaScript is also responsible for this. You can also use JavaScript for check forms, the creation of security passwords, special effects, and interactive gaming. It is used for building mobile phone apps, and for creating applications that are server-based. It is easy to add JavaScript to an HTML document simply by including snippets of code into your HEADER or BODY.

To be honest, the hardest part about learning to code in any language is actually getting started. Once you start, once you have learned all the basics, you will find it so much easier to move on to advanced programming.

JavaScript Mock Test

Most of the following questions cover what you have already covered in this book while a couple of them are just common sense. If you do not feel that you are ready to answer the questions just yet then do not hesitate to go back over the book and work through it again. Unlike the exercises in the book, I will be providing you with the answers to these questions.

When you are ready, make yourself comfortable and begin.

Question 1

Which of these statements are true about the features of JavaScript?

1. JavaScript was designed for the creation of applications that are network-centric
2. JavaScript is an interpreted lightweight programming language
3. JavaScript is integrated with and is complementary to java
4. All of these

Question 2

Which of the following HTML elements is JavaScript placed into?

1. <script>
2. <js>
3. <javascript>
4. <scripting>

Question 3

Which of the following is the right place for JavaScript to be inserted?

1. The <BODY> section
2. The <HEAD> section
3. Both the <BODY> and the <HEAD> sections

Question 4

Which of the following is the right syntax for when you want to reference an external script with the name of "xxx.js"?

1. <script name="xxx.js>
2. <script src="xxx.js">
3. <script href="xxx.js">

Question 5

Any external JavaScript file should have a <script> tag in it

1. True
2. False

Question 6

How would you write "Hello World" into an alert box?

1. alertBox('Hello World");
2. msgBox("Hello World");
3. alert("Hello World");
4. msg("Hello World");

Question 7

How do you start a WHILE loop?

1. while (i < = 10; i++)
2. while (i < = 10)
3. while (i = 1 to 10)

Question 8

Which of these statements is a valid function type supported by JavaScript?

1. Anonymous function
2. Named function
3. Both of these
4. None of these

Question

Which of these statements about callbacks is correct?

1. Some callbacks are only events, called so that the user can react when a specific state is triggered
2. A callback is nothing more than a simple JavaScript function that is

passed as an option or argument to a method
3. Both of these
4. None of these

Question 10

Which built-in method is used to return a number's value as a string representation?

1. toString()
2. toValue()
3. toNumber()
4. None of these

Question 11

Which of these Boolean object functions will return a string that contains the Boolean object source?

1. valueOf()
2. toSource()
3. toString()
4. None of these

Question 12

Which of these String object functions will return the characters in a specified string between two specified indexes in the string?

1. slice()
2. substr()
3. split()
4. substring()

Question 13

Which of these functions of string objects will create a string that is to be displayed in a large font just as if it were placed in a <big> tag?

1. big()
2. anchor()
3. italics()
4. blink()

Question 14

Which of these functions of string objects will cause the string to be displayed as a superscript, just as if it were in a <sup> tag?

1. small()
2. sub()
3. strike()
4. sup()

Question 15

Which of these functions of array objects will return a value of true if all the elements in the array satisfy the testing function specified?

1. every()
2. concat()
3. some()
4. push()

Question 16

Which of these functions of array objects will apply one function to two values in an array simultaneously, from right to left, to reduce it down to one value?

1. push()
2. pop()
3. reduceRight()
4. reduce()

Question 17

JavaScript is case sensitive

1. True
2. False

Question 18

An anonymous function may be passed to another function as an argument

1. True
2. False

Question 19

Which of these types of variable may only be seen from inside the function that it was defined in?

1. Local variable
2. Global variable
3. Both of these
4. None of these

Question 20

Which of the following built-in methods will sort the elements in an array?

1. changeOrder(order)
2. sort()
3. order()
4. None of these

Question 21

Which of these string object functions will cause a string to be displayed in a smaller font, just as it if were in a <small> tag?

1. small()
2. link()
3. sub()
4. sup()

Question 22

Which of these array object functions will reverse the order of an array's elements?

1. push()
2. reduce()
3. reverse()
4. reduceRight()

Conclusion

Once again, I would like to thank you for taking the time to read my guide. I hope that you now have a better understanding of JavaScript and how it all works. It really isn't too difficult to learn; the hardest part is getting started. So long as you have plenty of patience and time, and are willing to concentrate on what you are doing, you will soon be programming JavaScript like a pro.

Once you have the hang of the basics, you can move on to more advanced JavaScript topics and concepts – do not do this until you are certain you fully understand everything in this book. There are plenty of avenues for you to explore – forums that will give you the help you need, further education websites and plenty of tutorials, some free and some that you must pay for. And let's not forget the Internet is a wealth of useful information so make use of it to further your learning.

Please, do make use of the examples in the book. Try them out in your own JavaScript environment and use them to learn how the various elements of JavaScript work. The exercises are also a great way for you to practice what you learned, purely for your own peace of mind.

JavaScript is a fun language and, given that it is mainly for web development, you can create some truly stunning work with it. The best way to learn is to dive in and have fun – lots of it!

Good luck on your journey!

*I'd like to give you a **FREE e- book** as my gift to you just see the link below. No strings attached. :) (If you can't find your confirmation e-mail, try looking in your junk mail)

http://bit.ly/2yFU3B0

Simply as a 'thank you' for downloading this book, this link will give you free access to an exclusive service that will send you notifications when Amazon's Best sellers are released, and are on discount price or go on FREE promotion. If you are someone who is interested in saving a TON of money, simply click the FREE e- book link above.

As an added bonus...I would like to invite you to join my exclusive GROUP. You will be a part of a community of programming & technology experts/enthusiast.

The added benefit to this is you will have access to my most recent and newest bestselling books on the market for FREEE!

I have a new book coming out soon and you don't want to miss out!

Join my exclusive group by clicking the link below...

http://bit.ly/2gzY2c1

Join now

JavaScript Mock Test Answers

These are the answers to the question in the mock JavaScript test:

Question 1

Answer – 4. All of the above

Question 2

Answer – 1. <script>

Question 3

Answer – 3. Both the <BODY> and the <HEAD> sections are correct

Question 4

Answer – 2. <script src="xxx.js">

Question 5

Answer – 2. False. It is not necessary

Question 6

Answer – 3. alert("Hello World");

Question 7

Answer – 2. while (i < = 10)

Question 8

Answer – 3. Both of these

Question 9

Answer – 3. Both of the above are correct

Question 10

Answer – 1. toString()

Question 11

Answer – 2. toSource()

Question 12

Answer – 4. substring()

Question 13

Answer – 1. big()

Question 14

Answer – 4. sup()

Question 15

Answer 1. every()

Question 16

Answer – 3. reduceRight()

Question 17

Answer – 1. True

Question 18

Answer – 1. True

Question 19

Answer – 1. Local variable

Question 20

Answer – 2. sort()

Question 21

Answer – 1. small()

Question 22

Answer – 3. reverse()

Made in the USA
Middletown, DE
26 November 2017